C000082029

Rethinking InfoSec

Thoughts on why today's Information Security doesn't work, and how we can do better.

Greg van der Gaast

To truth and reason.

Table of Contents

Book Structure

Things got a little out of hand as I was writing this book. I had to whittle it down and eventually decided to break things out in multiple books rather than try and structure this one too much.

Yes, more of my rantings in the future, God help us.

I finally settled on an approach similar to how I've split my 3-day Information Security Leadership course and decided to break things down as follows:

Book 1, *Rethinking InfoSec* (this one), is a collection of ideas and concepts, of many semi-random thoughts covering an array of topics I hope will help you, which I've tried to structure in reasonably logical order.

It does not cover what most "CISO" or InfoSec books cover, such as standards and controls. There will be no tooling here. Just the mental, business, strategic, and human aspects that matter most to the role of proactive Information Security leadership.

Please note that some of this book is articles I've written previously. As such, certain examples may be repeated a few times, but usually in slightly different contexts so I've left them in. This is somewhat exacerbated by trying to group topics together logically as well since these repetitions may take place closer together. Bear with me.

Book 2, *Influencing InfoSec*, will focus on executive and strategic communication in depth. How to create strong internal traction through fanatical engagement to advance your objectives, and quite possibly your career.

Book 3, *Structuring InfoSec*, will be more about how to create an Information Security framework that's custom-fitted to our organisation, how to structure it, maintain it, get it supported by management and more.

I think I'll call the whole thing the "*InfoSec Leadership Series*".

Cheesy, I know.

Ironically, my original working title was "*Who Pwned my Cheese*", thanks to a brilliant idea by Jonathan Kempe. Unfortunately, amazon just kept trying to autocorrect that title.

Here we go.

Martin Scorsese

Before we start, I want to put to put forward a caveat.

I recently saw that there is an online "Masterclass" course on film-making by Martin Scorsese.

Martin does things his way, in his style, and is clearly doing something right because he's made some of the most loved and critically acclaimed films of the last 50 years. He's obviously a perfect candidate to give such a course.

Here's the thing: Some people freaking *hate* his movies.

And among those that enjoy his films, if you break it down to every individual viewer, there are things you could have changed to make the film more enjoyable to each one.

All this to say 2 things:

1. That you or others may not like or agree with my approach. I'm here to share what works for me. Often a lot of the resistance stems from simply being used to something else, so I urge the reader to try and forget about the existing thoughts they have as to not allow them to "railroad" their thinking.

Even if you find yourself disagreeing all the same, there are undoubtedly elements you can benefit from and add to your approach. My only warning here would be that if you can't do that then you're lacking the fundamental flexibility to be successful. Why? Because, as we'll cover extensively, hard approaches are one of the single biggest reasons Information Security fails in practice. Flexibility to each situation is key.

2. What I will be discussing is based on more than 20 years of *my* experience, across a specific set of organisations, times, cultures, management and delivery teams, etc. They will not be exactly like yours and, while some of the concepts presented here will be universal and others help you make the correct determinations, *you* are the person that is in the ideal position to best know your environment and therefore *you* should feel free to change and modify the approach to best work for yourself and *your* organisation.

It seems strange to say, but in some ways if you follow what I say in this book *exactly* then you'd be doing it wrong.

This book is about making us reflect as to how we can make the right decisions for ourselves in any given situation, situations in which I may not be able to tell you anything about without being there myself.

Making these decisions, doing what's right, whether it's something technical or human, is in many ways what InfoSec Leadership is about.

Another thing: Yes, I will be using lots of generalisations in this book. I'm often criticised for this by people trying to debunk what I'm saying.

Relax.

Take away what you need, what you can use, what inspires you. If something I say doesn't apply to some subset of your particular reality, just ignore it. Better yet, adapt it for your use, reinvent it, go nuts.

But, again, if you're just going to dismiss things I say without thinking them through, or working out how they could work for you, without considering if it has applications elsewhere, then you've missed the point and your thinking probably doesn't lend itself to the kind of mentality needed to perform in the world of practical Information Security.

I have a simple rule: take something away from interaction. You could think I'm the world's biggest idiot, but you should still be able to learn something, either from my thoughts or *your* [potentially opposing] thoughts sparked by mine.

Sadly, we live in a world where people love to be negative and criticise.

Every situation is different, I cannot speak to yours, but I hope you can relate some of the thoughts and examples in this book to your life and your work, even if only to be inspired by them to do something different still.

Most of all this book is about sharing thoughts, in the hope they are helpful to you.

To those that would rather nit-pick than gain something from the knowledge in this book, you're wasting your own time more than mine.

For those genuinely wanting to learn and better themselves, for the benefit of themselves and others, I hope I don't let you down.

If I can help in any other way, don't hesitate to get in touch.

The Electrical Box

This past year, in some of my talks, I've been using two analogies to explain why Information Security is so ineffective at stopping breaches and why the cost of doing it is spiralling out of control. It's the same reason.

The first analogy is about an electrical junction box.

Imagine your main junction box at home blows up. You call an electrician. They carefully examine the box for several minutes and determine it needs to be completely replaced and rewired. A week later it blows up again. You call them back. They replace it again. A week later it blows up again. This time they suggest spending a little more money on a beefier model. It blows up again, but after a month. Ah! Result! We go bigger, it blows up still, so we go bigger again. After a few iterations you end up with a massively expensive industrial junction box in your house, but it only blows up once a year.

Then someone with a slightly different mentality comes along. That "why is this *actually* happening, not limiting myself to just the box in front of my nose" mentality.

After 5 seconds this person turns around and asks you "How long has that water pipe up there been leaking onto the junction box?"

This happens every time I walk into an organisation.

Fortunes spent on mitigating problems caused by simple things we didn't consider to be "our" responsibility.

I first came up with this analogy when someone told me we shouldn't get involved in "IT" operations such as asset management and patching, that it's not our job, and that we shouldn't get "suckered" into doing that extra work.

But, it's those areas (or rather, defects in those areas) that create the vast majority of our SecOps workload. It's not "extra" work, it's an intelligent investment of effort to save tons of work *and* provide assurance.

Make no mistake about it, Equifax, Capital One, British Airways, and Travelex all could have been prevented entirely if they'd improved these "IT" processes.

Is our job to perpetuate a reactive security approach, or to actually keep things from being breached in the first place? For me it's the latter, and it's why I'll always proactively try to address as many issues as far upstream as I can. It's the only sustainable way, it's far more effective, and it carries a fraction of the cost.

I repeat: I believe that we, as security *professionals*, *must not* refuse to get involved in IT and business process when they cause the issues. Anything else is just lining the security industry's pockets at your organisation's expense. It is also dereliction of duty.

This is the danger of limiting our thinking, our scope. How we currently do security is difficult to unlearn, but we must remain inquisitive and curious in a holistic way and not limit ourselves to "our area."

Think bigger and be proactive. Make a difference rather than perpetuating a cycle.

The Car Factory

The second analogy is similar, but this time allows me to illustrate the shape the industry has taken a bit better.

Imagine you're standing on the sidewalk looking at a car factory.

To one side is a huge parking lot, a staging ground for the finished cars. To the other, the factory itself.

Parts and sheet metal get delivered to an assembly line in the building. The metal is stamped into bodies and painted. Engines, transmissions, suspension assemblies bolted into the bodies, interiors put together and screwed into place. A complex combination of tasks, resulting in a final finished product which is then pushed out of the factory building onto the parking lot.

From the 3rd floor.

The finished cars end up in the lot damaged, crumpled, and full of issues. People rush towards them, flip them back onto their wheels, cart them to a corner of the lot, assess the damage, figure out what they need to repair, order the parts, the necessary tools, and so forth.

But the crumpled cars keep coming, one after the other they fall from the 3rd floor of the factory. So we hire more people, then upgrade the tooling to work faster, buy a forklift so we can flip them and carry them off to work stations more easily, we set up workshops so we can work at all hours and in the rain, we start doing triage to break the issues down into different categories, cars with side damage, front end damage, drivetrain damage. We start allocating specific workshops and more specialised teams for each, we establish project management practices around the more complex jobs, set up workflows for cars that need multiple stations, hire more specialists and more managers to do and oversee all this work, we set up management systems and quality frameworks, bring in vendors for solutions, consultants, auditors, and so on.

Despite all this we have to queue and prioritise, to start implementing risk management practices to determine what's actually most important and what defects can we actually (hopefully) get away with because we simply can't do it all.

Maybe we'd even set up a bunch of conferences to talk about how we're doing. While we're at it, let's hand out some awards too from time to time?

Because, why not? I mean we've been burning ourselves out to build and run this amazing huge multi-billion-dollar ecosystem to get these cars sorted out.

Sure, we occasionally send one out that has a massive crash due to a defect we didn't spot or address, but some of them even turn out alright!

Meanwhile, the odd idiot (which fortunately is a *tiny* minority) can't help but think that not a single one of these people working so hard in the parking lot has thought about walking into the factory and asking if they'd terribly mind making assembly line terminate on the ground floor.

When such an idiot goes and asks those people in the parking lot why they don't, the idiot is told that they are experts and that he/she (the idiot) doesn't know anything about how this works. Maybe someone in the back will realise what the poor idiot means and shout at them, telling them it's not that easy.

Not that easy, ok. But surely it has to be easier than doing all of this?

And that's the issue with Indoctrination, and the sheer scale at which it has taken over the Information Security sector.

And that's my challenge as an apparent idiot.

This is the devolution I've seen taking place in the security industry over the last 20 years. Oddly, most people say the industry is "maturing."

Maturing? Ramping up the lunacy? An approach that, for obvious reasons, can't ever be effective?

Look at the picture below and tell me whether it feels like we're winning to you?

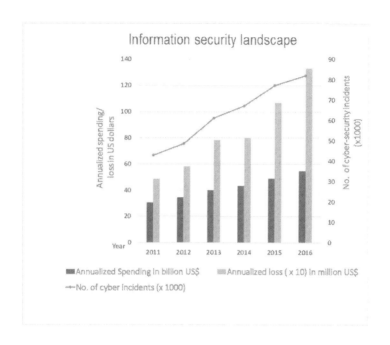

Information security landscape

Annualized Spending in billion US$ Annualized loss (x 10) in million US$
No. of cyber incidents (x 1000)

We're spending more and more, billions, and we're not even making a dent. Worse than that, the problem is running away from us. The current approach is simply hopeless. It's ineffective, expensive, and doesn't stand a chance.

Basic security, the kind that would have prevented virtually all the big breaches we see in the media, isn't hard. It isn't even nearly as complicated as we make it out to be. We just need to take a step back and address the real root causes.

17

Incremental Issues

Now, while the cars falling from the third floor is how I first thought up the analogy, and makes it a bit easier to present, the reality is that the cars aren't built perfectly and then launched from the third floor.

While the above adds some dramatic effect, a more realistic analogy would be that the cars go through dozens of stages during assembly and pick up incremental defects at many of them.

Let me give some examples.

Systems that aren't built to set and security-approved architectural standards.

Systems that *are* built to set and security-approved architectural standards, but security did a lousy job of the standards themselves, or didn't think the process through properly, or didn't maintain it.

Poor processes, period. Processes have to be well thought-out. They have to take into consideration numerous factors: who they will be executed by, with what, how, what could go wrong, how can they be made consistent, what could disturb them, what will they be covering, how will exceptions be covered, how will they be effectively reviewed and maintained, how can other processes reinforce them and vice-versa, etc.

I used to hate writing processes, but the fact is they are absolutely necessary. The problem is that I find organisations consistently have *terrible* poorly thought-out processes that are doomed to fail, miss things, or be ignored.

Your process creation exercise is your opportunity to review how things truly work, technically, organisationally, people-wise, etc. It's your chance to really get into details, to discover how things work, should work, and how you can reach that point in your particular organisation. Instead I usually see processes that are half a page to tick a box, or just generic templates and best practices that don't reflect their actual environment, people, or culture.

I once came across a firewall rule review process that was 6 lines long. That company, a large MSP doing billions in commercial and government business, turned out to have 45,000 (yes) undocumented firewall rules because things fell through the cracks. And that was with a single account/customer.

My revised process was 20 pages long, part of a made-to-measure framework, and part of that framework was continuous improvement procedures *and* an operational schedule for execution and review.

It's important to note the process wasn't any longer to execute (in fact, things had been made much easier – it was clearer) it's just that it went into details about different scenarios and clarified the approach so that things would be sustainable and auditable in a straight-forward way.

We have to care enough to take the time to do things properly. We could get away with minimal effort and tick-boxing requirements, but long-term we'll create more work to maintain it and we'll never have delivered value or assurance.

Make no mistake about it, it's a battle of integrity versus entropy, and safeguarding the consistency of your assembly line and your maintenance processes is critical to not getting stuck in the parking lot scenario.

Proactivity

I dislike the term "Risk Management."

I feel in many cases it means "risk juggling." It is, in many places, almost the opposite of securing.

When I say "securing" I mean actually securing the systems, fundamentally, proactively.

Proactivity is something I think we're sorely lacking. Once again this is a "scope" thing as far as our thinking goes because many people believe they are being proactive, but they are doing so within a narrow scope that doesn't extend far enough. They would benefit from taking a step back to take a look at the bigger picture.

I once made the following post on LinkedIn:

I'm told, by knowledgeable people whom I respect, that just making things secure is impossible. That you have to focus on managing risk instead. I'm sorry, but...

-Patching systems is not impossible.
-Hardening systems before deployment is not impossible.
-Maintaining configurations on live systems is not impossible.
-Being thorough in your CM to avoid introducing vulnerabilities into production is not impossible.
-Enforcing architectural standards is not impossible.
-Knowing where your data sits is not impossible.

-Getting involved in projects and development (Or anywhere else!) is not impossible.
-Improving security mechanisms around applications to fit their usage is not impossible.
-Unified and *accurate* asset management is not impossible
-Logging and correlating properly is not impossible.
-Getting rid of blind-spots in hierarchy and silos is not impossible.
-Mentoring people to be proactive on all of the above is not impossible.
-Having the curiosity to dig and find the issues and trace their root causes is not impossible.
-Building the relationships to get others to help you resolve the issues is not impossible.

Let's take a step back from what we think we know and try.

Even if it means doing more than our "fair share", let's do it anyway.

Thoughts?

The backlash was tremendous.

I would put it into 2 categories.

The first category were genuinely smart and highly capable people (that I respect) struggling to see the argument from my point of view. Stuck with the idea that doing better means more work and more cost.

The following comment I received illustrates this well:

Good points. But also very exhausting when budget is limited, resource is limited, growth takes over everything, and human mistakes are considered in the loop. This is right, but leads to burn out. I definitely agree, but also realise that this is nearly impossible to be achieved properly.

But... being proactive leads to *fewer* recurring issues, fewer headaches, fewer costs, fewer resources needed, and better scalability. We need to shift the thinking further upstream and on a broader strategic timescale. The failure to do this is crippling the productivity and impact (in terms of delivering assurance) of some truly great people in InfoSec.

As for the human mistakes mentioned, these are just another issue to address proactively.

The second category was more defensive, calling, well, "bullshit" on the idea of proactive behaviour, refusing to even accept that there may be different angles from which to approach the problem.

Maybe angle isn't the right term, because we can see more from the same angle if we step back and have a wider view. Unfortunately, our thinking, scope, and vision

– how close we are to the problem – is often limited by the status quo.

This second category illustrates the detrimental power of indoctrination and blame culture, as well as why positivity and humility, which forces us to learn and grow, are *so* important.

At the time I had used yet another analogy to try and illustrate what I meant with proactivity.

Imagine if our problem wasn't preventing security breaches, but rather dealing with a viral disease.

(Covid-19 outbreak at time of writing is purely coincidental!)

Let's say people are getting sick by the tens or hundreds of thousands, so we need to build and staff a thousand hospitals dedicated to this disease.

Let's say 50% of people will be hit by the disease and we can save 95% of those, meaning nearly 98% (97.5%) of the population survives.

Objectively, 98% is a decent success rate and can be seen as a solid benchmark to maintain.

Or, we can ask *why* these people are getting sick. The answer? "Because they were near other sick people!"

Ok, great, but why did they get sick? "Well they also were near *other* sick people!"

Ok, great, but why were *they* sick? "Well because they *also* were near other sick people, obviously. What are you? A moron?"

This is what dealing with indoctrination is like.

Eventually someone has an epiphany and realises this might be a virus and we could possibly vaccinate people.

A simple vaccine eliminating the need for containment and treatment since a vaccinated person wouldn't get sick and could merrily walk among a crowd of infected people without issue.

It's also a lot cheaper to vaccinate someone than to treat someone. Yes, we're currently only treating 50% of people and you'd have to vaccinate 100% of people. But that's not twice the work is it?

We may be vaccinating twice as many people, but each one is less than $1/100^{th}$ the effort of treating them after they get the disease.

Plus, while not instantaneous, it's not going to take too long before far fewer hospital resources are needed, so it's worth making that extra bit of effort up front. And yet, because it's "extra" effort we often tend to say we don't have the capacity, yet happily end up doing 50 times more work on the long term.

Now it's important to note that the doctors and nurses and equipment manufacturers and managers that run the hospitals all feel they're doing the right thing, but really all their lobbying for more resources to help fund those hospitals is taking attention and resource away from a far simpler way to solve the problem.

Indoctrination, emotional investment, and economics have set in, the scope of thinking has been narrowed, and it's now very difficult to get people to consider the cost-effectiveness of different approaches that would replace what they're currently doing.

Time and time again in the comments and discussion that followed my post was the argument that Risk Management was about balancing resources, providing the assurance the company could afford.

In our analogy, this would equate to balancing the costs at the hospitals to provide the best service we can offer for the limited budget.

But I am not talking about hospitals at all. I am talking about vaccinating, which is orders of magnitudes cheaper than building hospitals. Sure, it would still be good measure to build a couple of hospitals to catch the odd case. But 2 would be plenty, we no longer need a thousand. Vaccinating everyone and funding 2 hospitals (even running them at an absolute peak cost & quality level) is still going to be a lot cheaper than building and funding 1,000 hospitals, even mediocre ones.

If we address the areas that cause our fundamentals issues, such as user training, asset management, patching, system hardening/provisioning, monitoring, and vulnerability management, to go from, say, 95% up to 99.5% effective, we can massively reduce our reliance on reactive security (pretty much everything we consider Security Operations today). After all, going from 5% exposure to 0.5% exposure is a tenfold decrease and can be achieved by using engagement rather than funding.

Go back through the list of things I said were impossible and come up with proactive solutions. I'll give you a hint: think long-term and think of what you could do if you'd built traction and influence throughout the organisation.

Let me give you an example with the first one:

-Patching systems is not impossible.

Immediately people will say "Ah but some systems are end of life, and some are legacy and can't be maintained!"

Ok, but why do you have legacy systems? Why has stuff fallen behind? What can you do *now* to stop this from happening in the future? Also, that legacy system will *eventually* be replaced, just like every other system, so start working out how you can make sure all future systems will be designed and deployed taking patching and [security] maintenance in mind and implement it. That's how you make sure you have fewer issues in the future, by addressing things now, even if you won't see the result until years down the line.

Now go through the other scenarios and figure out how. It doesn't matter how long it will take to sort them out, all can be done with relatively little effort given enough *influence* and a long enough timeframe.

Trimming Trees

Thought I'd share an article I wrote some time ago about how issues tend to branch out if not addressed.

The "issue tree" is a term that I came up with to describe one of the core problems with the Information Security status quo.

Picture a big sturdy tree trunk. Then out of that come 5 or 6 large branches. Then each of those branches has 10 or more branches, then each of those has a few more not insignificant branches, and each of those sprouts more small offshoots than you can count. You end up with thousands of branches.

Now imagine each one of those branches is an issue. And the reason each one sprouts into more is because, just like branches, not properly addressing an issue and allowing it to persist (grow) leads to more issues.

In Information Security we need to have controls around those issues. But, for some reason, we insist on not addressing fundamentals and waiting for those 5-6 essential areas (our first big branches coming off the trunk) to become a thousand branches, all over the organisation, each requiring slightly different solutions, usually several organisational layers away from where we are and our direct control.

At this level, even the solutions we employ sprout little branches of their own: Resources have to be taken from somewhere to operate them, plus we now have to manage not just their operation, but their upkeep, configuration, certificates, etc. It all results in simply too many things to maintain visibility and control over. You end up spending more time managing security tools than providing any improvement in actual security.

All you have to do is look at InfoSec job listings to see the truth in this. We're looking for *far* more people that can handle tools than people that actually have *fundamental* security-minded thinking. Heck the latter have been replaced completely in some areas.

Example: We put little effort into system builds or effective patching, then expect budget to increase SOC capacity to handle the resulting incidents. See many job listings for process improvement skills? How about Incident Response and SOC analysts? Exactly.

The real danger is that it's not just expensive having to control 1,000's of branches, it's also exhausting and *unsustainable*. Things will get through the cracks, and breaches will happen.

We must focus on the core branches closer to the trunk and control them before they sprout more issues.

In an ideal world you could solve the large majority of InfoSec issues with the following 4 actions:

1. Develop interpersonal relationships. Talk with your people. Whether they be developers, architects, InfoSec, or regular users. Help them understand you and guide their work to take security into account. And let them help *you* understand what really goes on in your organisation. It is almost certainly not whatever your reporting says.

2. Make sure systems are provisioned cleanly, architected properly, deployed in an up-to-date state with regards to patching and configuration standards, and that they can be updated/maintained/patched and that those relevant processes are in place and effective.

3. Produce clean and tested code not susceptible to common software bugs such as buffer overflows, race conditions, etc. No more bugs, vulnerabilities, patches, exploits. Magic. This is especially true of internal and enterprise applications.

4. Now that you have solid systems and applications, ensure systems and access are configured properly and *consistently* over time. No point in building Fort Knox if you leave the windows open.

Yes, fixing such fundamental things so far away from the InfoSec department, especially those around improving the code base, might seem remote and a little unrealistic, but we can try.

Even if imperfect, we may just find that if we start implementing some standards today, the picture may be improved beyond all expectations in a few years' time.

But we're not really doing these things at all and, as a result, businesses now have thousands of separate points that need information security technologies and processes around them.

It's not going to change until we take the initiative. Sadly, we're not and remain with the reactive approach dealing with thousands of branches. Worse still, we allow them to multiply further.

This is expensive and doomed to fail for the simple reason that it's just too much to manage without sacrificing levels of visibility and quality. That loss of visibility will eventually lead to those security solutions becoming ineffective or failing completely, often without [InfoSec] management's knowledge.

This is why layering on more and more new flavour of the month technologies cannot work. To add insult to injury, vendors and industry "experts" are now shifting to a stance that says "You can't keep them out, it's too complex, you have to prioritise and focus instead on detection and response!"

Sod off. You're the ones causing the complexity.

If you'd focused less than half as much effort at a lower level, by which I mean upstream, where you only still had 5-10 branches, in order to keep them from branching into thousands, you wouldn't have to worry about prioritising, you'd have ample resources to have near perfect control.

The solution to effective information security, while for some reason elusive to what is set to become a quarter-trillion-dollar security industry (*cough* sales *cough*), is dead simple: Don't let the issue tree grow to where you have an absolutely impossible number of branches to manage. Keep it trim.

Effective architecture that takes into account your entire estate, a secure SDLC, a well-defined operational framework, clear build standards, effective provisioning, secure consolidated IT management tools and, above all, InfoSec management that talks with everyone, so they can address the real issues and not whatever some bogus reporting says.

Imagine if you had code development standards that meant your code wasn't subject to buffer overflows or other vulnerabilities. Imagine if your architecture meant you could have consistent and easy to maintain access controls. Imagine you had IT management tooling and processes that ensured systems were clean and every OS, application, and database ran with least privilege. Imagine if your patching was automatic and completed within 24 hours of patches being available, including testing, because your infrastructure was designed accordingly?

The vast majority of InfoSec work is either finding and remediating known vulnerabilities or responding to incidents caused by their presence.

We know what these vulnerabilities are, we can figure out what causes them. Fix *that*. It's easier and far cheaper than sitting in a SOC all day catching the resulting incidents and opening tickets to sort missing patches and misconfigurations that never should have been.

No environment can be perfect, you will still have a handful of issues. But that's few enough that you can address them, comprehensively, with the best technologies, and by creating solid processes and procedures for your organisation. And that last part is only possible when you have so few issue branches that you have the time to make sure they're addressed perfectly instead of running around like a headless chicken trying to keep dozens of different security systems running (and missing most of what's actually going on).

I can't think of a single fundamental security technology that's come out in the past ten years that addresses a problem that couldn't essentially have been eliminated by sorting root causes. The problem, perhaps, is that it requires a skillset, a degree of thought effort, and a level of involvement that the now nearly ubiquitous information security industry indoctrination doesn't allow. Let's change that.

Now, please, stop burning through cash, stop layering the latest "fix-everything" technology over last year's "fix-everything" technology. No amount of AI, or correlation, or canned user awareness, or incident response, or <insert latest tech here>, or appliances of any genre is going to be as effective as shaping your issue tree to where you only have a handful of issues that can be easily and cost-effectively covered.

Ground Floor, Please

Totally different topic: How should we manage InfoSec? Bottom up? Top Down?

Management is hard to define. Should an InfoSec Manager (or Head of InfoSec, CISO, or whatever) be technical? Be more managerial? Both? Is that even possible?

Better yet, is it even relevant? Is this pigeonholing perhaps a gross oversimplification that's leading us to miss the point completely? Do we even know what's needed for optimal InfoSec leadership?

I see "technical" types just hammering away at incidents and, sometimes, vulnerabilities, in a way that will never stem the tide of new issues coming their way, missing the big picture in a myopic approach to security. Some are technically brilliant, implementing the very latest IT and security technologies, in elegant solutions, on time, on budget. But the reality is that you cannot do information security *management* without building relationships, without promoting understanding, without collaboration, without identifying root causes of why things happen (and *root* causes are rarely technical). Fixing ground-level issues will not make a dent into the nearly unlimited cultural, procedural, awareness, and other issues you have that are breeding the problems.

You cannot fix it from the ground, after the issues have already hit you. You need to get upstream, ahead of the current. You need to manage it from the top.

Except, with the traditional management approach, that doesn't work either.

Ah the management types... With their ISO this and ITIL that, focused more on abstract compliance than security, and putting out policies without the faintest idea of what is going on at the ground level.

Having decisions driven by data and reporting that almost never conveys the real picture, something they're blissfully unaware of.

I've seen it all; reports showing environments as squeaky clean while they are bordering on criminal negligence. Sometimes people in operations thought issues were false positives when they weren't and didn't report them. Sometimes the savvier ones saw the technical truth but are told by their line managers to keep quiet and report just how good of a job they were doing to the CISO or to the client... while the whole shebang could fall over at any moment.

Cumbersome compliance without any real security is bad enough, it's even worse when it adds the *illusion* of security.

Pushing down a strategy that branches out as it goes down the organisation (as it should) and eventually reaching operations is a sound approach. The problem is that no matter how well intended senior management is, with layers of reporting filtering out crucial details (losing the "feel" of the situation), their strategy will almost always miss the real problems, simply because they won't even know what they are. In some cases, the problem is the very people reporting up to them, whether unwittingly, or, in the worst cases, maliciously. You can't identify the targets from 50,000 feet. It takes direct understanding of what's going on at the ground level and no PowerPoint presentation or report is going to help you there.

So, what's the answer?

If you're going to develop a proactive strategy, you need to push it down from the top, but you need intimate awareness of who does what on the bottom to make sure you have the right strategy that delivers what the people need in a way they can use.

I do assessments the same way; start at the bottom find a loose thread (any issue) and pull until you get to the top. You will find more disconnected management, policy, and broken process than you can imagine, for the simple reason they never took the time to put the reality together before pushing the "solution" down.

Know what goes on "down there" and then craft the right top-down approach that's both accurate and prescriptive enough to address the issues.

Secure Like a Hacker

When I started out (as just a teenager securing his machine, so his hard drive wouldn't be formatted within 5 minutes of joining some hacking channel on IRC), IDS was little more than packet sniffing with some rules and firewalls were nothing but port blocking.

All we'd use to secure our machines were the operating system's features, nothing more.

We'd strip services back to what was needed, bring patching up to date, eliminate unnecessary permissions, made sure services such as web servers and databases were configured well, sometimes tweak some code libraries.

You didn't need anything else, and it worked.

And it would have prevented the majority of large breaches happening today. British Airways, Equifax, Capital One, Travelex, etc.

So why have we given up on this approach and left things to fall apart? Why did we start focusing more exclusively on the perimeter instead of thoroughly securing systems and then, when we finally realised the perimeter-focused approach didn't work, turned our attention to a "detect and respond" model that's possibly even less effective?

I see surveys nowadays saying most CISOs would rather focus on detection and response than protection.

I find that absolutely ridiculous.

Sure, all these things have *some* value, but we should be securing proactively from the inside out, from each host to each perimeter, not *reactively* from the outside in.

This is the same reason why penetration testing will never offer sustainable solutions if we don't also look into the true root causes of the findings. Oh, you had a misconfiguration, or missing patch. Well fix your architectural standards, project lifecycle, and patching processes *once* instead of endlessly fixing one-off issues.

People say it's too much effort. No, it's less effort, certainly over time.

I think we stopped "securing like a hacker" when we entered the business reality. It wasn't just systems anymore, but people and business process and us geeks didn't really know how to handle those. We started working *around* them instead.

First, we stopped focusing on their systems and took on the perimeter instead, to try to protect whatever security nightmare lived inside. And now we play with all the fancy toys supposed to detect and respond to what's going on in there.

The thing is, we've never tried to actually get the skills to engage those people and the business, to enable us to evolve the original 70-ton tank* approach. We could still set up the systems themselves to be secure *and* perfectly fitted to the business requirements and how people work, but that would involve talking to people... The horror.

The irony of our new, very expensive, "detect and respond"-focused model is that it's not just less effective, but it has a fatal flaw: We can't detect things (through technical means) in areas that have fallen outside the scope of our monitoring. And this happens often because we frequently simply aren't aware of parts of the business. And that's down to the same inability to engage the people and the business which, if we had, would allow us to proactively secure things in the first place.

It's what happened to BA and Equifax. They simply weren't aware of what they even needed to secure, so those areas were ignored by their multi-million-pound/dollar security programmes, leaving them exposed to simple and common vulnerabilities.

*You really don't care who is throwing rocks at you when you drive a 70-ton tank, and when they hit you not much happens.

Technical Truth: Integrity

Touching on the last chapter, I'd like to talk about integrity, system's integrity, as one of the most basic tenets of Information Security. Let's go way back to basics for a moment.

Integrity is one of the CIA triad. In order to ensure the other two, Confidentiality and Availability, real-world systems first need *Integrity*.

Access controls and other technologies that ensure confidentiality require *integrity*. Preventing the system from being disabled or made unavailable also depends, to some measure, on *integrity*.

Now let's add that attacks on computer systems involve attack surface. Essentially any element of the system an attacker can potentially interact with and cause the system to deviate from what we intend its behaviour to be.

Let's look at the most fundamental disconnects of the current approach.

What we are trying to achieve?

Compliance to an outside standard? Installing "security" technology and academic frameworks? That's what most people think we're doing.

But what I want to do is for systems to be structured securely, to have *integrity*, and for the mechanisms that enable that integrity to work as intended.

This is where we fail; because systems are being designed poorly. We then design "controls" *around* them (this is the typical scope of work for most Information Security organisations). But these controls are typically tick-box exercises and done with a significant lack of care and no holistic thinking.

These controls also suffer from the same issue with integrity; If you don't secure the systems they run on top of, what's the point? They cannot achieve greater integrity than what they are running on top of. Putting layers of security on top of a foundation that cannot guarantee integrity is essentially an exercise in futility. It's at the very least a fundamentally flawed approach.

How can I trust any data in a SIEM that's running on an end of life unpatched server? I can't, yet I see this kind of thing all the time.

Let's start with how systems get exploited and introduce the following fundamental terms: (yes, *really* basic)

- Attack surface

- Vulnerable attack surface
- Patching
- Hardening

Attack surface is any exposed area of a system, from open TCP/IP ports on a system, to an end user, whether known to be vulnerable or not.

Vulnerable attack surface is any such surface that has an element of vulnerability.

For example, a service running on one of the aforementioned ports (such as a web server presenting a website) that could allow an attacker to trick the service into granting them access or performing some other beneficial action.

I once compromised a system that had an email service by tricking that service into sending an undeliverable email to the system's password file where account details are kept.

Part of the body of the email contained a line containing a username and password of my own creation, creating an entry in the password file granting me complete access to the system. I then merely had to log into the system with my own credentials, the system then looked them up in its password file, found them, validated my password, and gave me full access.

These vulnerabilities are regularly discovered and resolved through software fixes. I.e. updates and patches.

This brings us to *patching*. Clearly it is important for us to install these patches and updates in order to not be vulnerable. It is the biggest and simplest way we can reduce our vulnerability.

If your systems are fully patched up, we can say we are more than reasonably secure against attacks that would exploit those vulnerabilities. Most attacks and "exploits" that exploit known vulnerabilities appear well after the patches for those vulnerabilities become available. It's critical to apply them quickly, but most organisations are months and years behind. Not only are they running behind, but some systems are missed completely due to poor process, poor tooling, or a lack of awareness as to the systems' very existence.

Beyond patching there is a further step we can take to secure individual systems: *Hardening*.

Hardening can mean limiting the less secure functionalities of a specific service so that any vulnerability in that subcomponent cannot be used. For example, even though the mail server I mentioned earlier was running an old unpatched version with a vulnerability, disabling the functionality that allowed forwarding undeliverable mail to an internal file would have prevented me from compromising the system in the way that I did. Hardening could have prevented that breach even if they were behind on the patching.

This can further strengthen the security of a service, or increase the likelihood that, should a vulnerability be discovered in the future, we won't be affected by it. In some cases, it can even be used to remove vulnerabilities from older unsupported and otherwise vulnerable systems. It reduces our exposure in many ways and is always a good idea. Again, no specialised "security" tooling is needed.

These simple concepts are the basic elements that allow us to make systems reasonably secure.

Naturally we must also apply access controls, role-based permissions, and, ideally, other layers of host security, as well as monitoring at the network level. But if we do not implement the basics above we can have no foundation on which to build security because the system will be open to compromise and all components and mechanisms we build on top of them can be likely be circumvented.

Patching and hardening of systems are very basic things. So basic that many information security professionals almost ignore them, leaving them up to IT. They'll often put them in place with a lame policy but virtually never dig to ensure that they are being done effectively.

Instead they go to trending and sexier technologies, but all these rely on a foundation, and they fail because of the lack of that foundation. You'd think we'd learn but instead of fixing that foundation the market tries to build yet more "solutions" to layer on top of the last failure.

Back to square one.

The security and trust of systems is based on their integrity. Nothing we build on top of them can compensate for the lack of integrity of the underlying system/layer. A compromise of that system compromises all elements that run on that system, whether they be applications or other security tools.

Systems security is primarily about maintaining that integrity, by building them cleanly to establish it, and then maintaining them to prevent entropy. If there is no vulnerable attack surface, a system cannot be compromised. Build and maintain them accordingly, it cannot be fixed via security add-ons.

I refer to my 70-ton tank analogy. You can be surrounded by 500 people with stones, guns, and angry crocodiles all hell bent to come after you, but if you're in a 70-ton tank – if you have integrity – nothing will hurt you.

Integrity. Make it a priority.

Bottle Caps

I always buy the milk jug with the collapsed neck, the can of soup with the dent in it, the crumpled cereal box, the banana with a couple spots.

If there's an item I need, and I see there's one where the packaging isn't perfect, I will buy that one. Because I know many other people won't just due to the damaged packaging, and it'll go to waste, despite the product being perfectly good. That means crops wasted, water wasted, animals slaughtered for nothing, emissions from transport, and all kinds of little impacts.

Most of these impacts will be far away, but they'll be there, and I know it because I've made a habit of thinking about and wanting to understand the full cycle of things. I despise waste and want to make that complete cycle, as a whole, as positive, effective, and efficient as possible.

Plus, just like global warming, the little things add up and before you know it you're in real trouble: Start neglecting security here and there (or even the tiniest details in security processes) and after a few years you're also going to be in a serious pickle.

We have to give a damn about the big picture to do the right things. Globally and in every small instance (though there may be some strategic prioritisation due to finite resources).

One of the things about me, long before I had any soft skills or was any good with people at all, was that I was *ridiculously* obsessed with how things worked together.

On a massive scale.

I thought of how things would impact other things to the point of taking the caps off of plastic bottles before recycling them when I was little.

Why? So that the *air* in them wouldn't go to waste should the bottle for whatever reason not get melted down. I'd imagine the outside air in the future being more polluted, while we had clean air trapped in plastic bottles in a landfill somewhere. Ridiculous, but not untrue. Of infinitesimally small impact, but still considered.

Now, apply that kind of obsessive mentality with technology [*and how people work with it*] and you really start coming up with interesting ways to enforce integrity and keep the entropy that threatens it at bay.

Think detailed, think big.

The Importance of Strategic Thinking

Referring back to my car factory analogy, I said one of the reasons we were stuck in the parking lot scope of thinking is that we were looking at what was directly in front of us.

It's like the water level is rising in a village of 2,000 people and every one of its inhabitants is busy taking all their possessions up to the second floor to spare them from the rising water.

Meanwhile, a crack is forming in the dam up the river that will cause it to collapse and wash away the entire village.

The irony is that it would only take 5% of the village's population of 2,000 to fix the dam, but they're too busy bringing their TVs upstairs to realise their whole damn (no pun intended) house and everything in it is about to be washed away and lost.

This is why it's so important to consider the entire picture, and to set objectives over *time*. A reasonable but not insignificant amount of time.

I can use X resource to address 2,000 issues per day, purely reactively (SecOps anyone?) and 3 years from now still be dealing with 2,000 issues per day. Or, more likely, even more.

Alternatively, I can take some of my resource away from these reactive roles, meaning we're only able to deal with, say, 1,800 of the issues now, but in 3 years' time that resource we put towards proactive activities will have reduced the number of daily issues from 2,000 to 200.

Meaning more and more of that formerly reactive resource is now free and can be reassigned towards further proactive measures and increasing our maturity level, creating a snowball effect of improvements, and extra capacity without increasing resource.

Information Security Skills Gap? More like surplus...

That said, initially it will look like you are doing *less* because you're only dealing with 1,800 vs 2,000 issues per day, and these are the metrics people see (one more reason metrics, at least many of the ones we use today, can be highly misleading). This is why it's so important to communicate the benefit of the strategic approach.

Fortunately, it's logical and quite simple to explain to most management teams. It's certainly easier than explaining what that big expensive SOC does all the time.

Plus, boards love strategic planning. It gives the impression you know what you're doing.

What does worry me is that many CISO's "strategic" plans are how to build and ramp up reactive capability (security tools, SOCs, bodies, 3rd party compliance standards around managing that reactive approach, etc.), rather than a proactive ever-improving (and cost-reducing) approach.

I suggest you think in terms of reducing issues, not ramping up security capacity. One is sustainable and cheap, the other one isn't. This can be clearly seen from industry figures where spend is going up and up both in absolute terms and % of IT budgets, all without ever slowing down the frequency of breaches.

Set yourself a goal state for the environment as you'd like to see it in 3-4 years. Again, not with X tools and a big SOC and loads of analysts, but of how IT and business processes need to be in order to have so few issues that you can manage tens of thousands of users with just a handful of resource.

And to be clear, I don't mean give yourself 3-4 years to fix all the individual vulnerabilities/problems. I mean fix the processes or lack of processes that resulted in those problems existing in the first place. Doing that first will give you the capability to remediate faster later, but you often won't even have to because all those issues will eventually be sorted through regular process (once you get those good processes in place) rather than remediation.

The larger your organisation is, the more effectively this works.

Giving yourself the time also takes off the pressure. You have a destination and plenty of time to get there. You should see roadblocks as redirection and milestones. They show you the way.

By the way, a strategic approach is not just less stressful, but also more psychologically rewarding because it means working with people and developing fruitful relationships.

Home Field Advantage

No InfoSec or Leadership book would be complete without a Sun Tzu quote, so here we go:

Know thy enemy.
Know thyself.
A thousand battles.
A thousand victories.

It's the second line that jumped out at me when I first heard it.

We've all heard the argument that the attacker only has to get it right once whereas we have to get it right every single time.

But if we think about it more closely, the attacker can only be right when *we* do something wrong, or *we* omit something. An attack or exploit, no matter how valid, cannot work if we've protected against it. And when we're talking about attacks that exploit a vulnerability due to a misconfiguration or missing patch, we need only get it right *once* to render a thousand attacks against that particular avenue ineffective.

This is my 70-ton tank analogy: You really don't care who's throwing rocks at you when you're driving a tank, and it's why proactively securing should trump things like threat intelligence, and detection and response in terms of priority. Those things are critical when your vehicle is made of thin sheet metal and glass, but irrelevant when it's made of 3-inch-thick hardened steel. The best part? This kind of armour, in our world, is free.

Another way of thinking of it is that we have the home field advantage.

In order to leverage it, you need to know it. We can't defend assets or mitigate attacks against weaknesses we don't know we have. If we spent half the time we spend on learning all the tech and intel and frameworks *out there*, on actually getting to know *our own* organisation so that we can fortify it correctly, our overall level of assurance would be much improved.

We can't do it as long as we're too busy focusing almost exclusively on the enemy (or on what other people think we should do, for that matter).

Instead of trying to catch the people running through our house every single time, let's learn where the doors, windows, and other avenues of entry are and focus on securing them. Sure, we do this to some degree, but we need to get better at it, because what we *think* we know about is rarely everything.

When I do assessments in companies, the speed and ease with which I find elements the security teams never bothered enquiring about is downright worrisome. It's frankly absurd and makes it easy for the law firms that typically ask me to run these assessments to argue negligence.

There's no point in spending a fortune on layering 20 layers of security tools/controls and then ignore the content on the website that's been hosting malicious code harvesting people's credit cards for ages. (You know who you are.)

It's pointless. If you never discover your own home turf because you never spoke to the business stakeholders, then you will fail.

The fact that security assumes every part of the business would be perfectly integrated and appear in your CMDB or whatever is *hilarious* – that'll never happen, it's on you to find out the true story.

The bottom line is this: If you look at most of the big breaches making headlines, it was the failure to *know thyself* that resulted in the compromise. The failure to leverage the home field advantage.

Leadership

I want to share with you a little story I read over the holidays.

General Krulak, former Commandant of the Marine Corps, would bake hundreds of cookies with his wife the week before Christmas every year.

On Christmas day at about 4am, he would drive himself to every Marine guard post in the Washington DC area and deliver Christmas cookies to Marines who were pulling guard duty that day.

One year, he had gone down to Quantico as one of his stops to the Marines on guard duty. He went to the command centre and gave a package to the Lance Corporal who was on duty.

He asked, "Who's the officer of the day?" The Lance Corporal said, "Sir, it's Brigadier General Mattis."

He spotted a cot in the room. He said, "No, Lance Corporal. Who slept in that bed last night?"

The Lance Corporal said, "Sir, it was Brigadier General Mattis."

About that time, General Krulak said that General Mattis came in, in a duty uniform with a sword, and General Krulak said, "Jim, what are you doing here on Christmas day?"

General Mattis told him that the young officer who was scheduled to have duty on Christmas day had a family, and he decided it was better for the young officer to spend Christmas Day with his family.

Krulak said, when telling this story, "That's just the kind of officer and person that Jim Mattis is. A Leader."

So, what is leadership? Well, I'm not even sure I'm qualified to say, but it certainly is *not* "being a boss."

To me I guess it's about figuring out the situation, the objective, working out the best way forward, and doing so as holistically as possible. It's not just about technical problems, but politics, organisations, personal relationships, understanding history, knowing what is likely to work, having the courage to admit when something doesn't, and the humility to learn from it.

And people. Caring about people. Wanting what's best for them well beyond what we need from them to get the job done. Helping them prepare for what they want to achieve even if it means they'll be leaving us.

(We'll have a chat about retention later on, because holding on to people that would rather go by giving them more money makes no sense to me, as does worrying about making them overqualified for their current role thinking they'll leave. If you're willing to let them leave, giving them all the tools and tutelage and skills to do so, chances are the best ones will still want to stay.)

I've realised that It's also about something a little different, and it's something I'm proud to say I've noticed about myself long before it had anything to do with leadership.

It's giving a damn about the greater good, about the big picture and the details. In the General Mattis story above, a subordinate Marine of much lower rank had a family and Mattis just felt it was more important that the Marine spend time with it, so he sacrificed his Christmas.

He thought beyond himself and did something you could argue is actually completely logical rather than based on character (it makes more sense for a young man with a family to spend time at home than Mattis who is unmarried and has no children). Completely logical in the greater picture, but not to his benefit. He did it anyway. And that's where the character comes in.

If we don't have this level of altruism, this level of leadership, then we need to get there.

Nothing will motivate us more than the desire to do the right thing for others. And nothing makes people want to listen and follow what you say more than displaying leadership.

Stop Being a CISO

No, really, stop. I think one of the best things you can do to be a good CISO is to stop being a "CISO."

What do I mean?

I'm involved in a lot of CISO discussion groups, events, round tables, dinners, etc. I'm usually the odd one out shrugging his shoulders because I simply don't do (or barely spend any time at all doing) the vast majority of things that consume their time.

I see endless discussions about what seems to be 4 main topics. Let's go through them.

The first is discussing and comparing GRC tools, calculating metrics, and how to scare the board into funding.

It's not that I spend a little less time doing this and a little more time doing something else; I simply don't bother with any of that stuff. At all. I just can't be arsed. There's more important things I can be doing to actually boost information assurance and help the organisation, and I can bypass all this time-consuming formality and bureaucracy around metrics just by having taken the time to establish personal relationships with the right people instead.

I can literally pull far more accurate and meaningful numbers out of the air and back them up as needed while in front of the board because, while most CISOs spend a huge chunk of their time plugging in arbitrary numbers into GRC tools trying to get an output that looks decent, I've instead been directly dealing and talking with the business and discovering what's actually happening on the ground. This means I can speak to it, the board recognises that fact, and trusts me.

More about this later in the *Metrics* chapter.

The second thing is Frameworks, being discussed like the latest fashion accessory, or how you should accessorise hot pants at the gym. Don't get me started. So much time is spent comparing and talking about experiences and outcomes of various 3rd party frameworks that they could have all developed a framework from scratch that actually suited their business with time to spare.

Oh! There's a novel idea. More on that later.

The third thing I see many CISOs spend a huge chunk of their time dealing with and discussing is current events. Stuff like possible increased hacking activity from some nation state or a critical patch to a dangerous vulnerability having just been released. I see them get busy seeking advice on how to proceed, how to best do it, how to convince stakeholders and executives that "This one is *really* important, and we *really* need to deploy it."

I just scratch my head asking why they haven't already made all of this stuff operational, standard, gotten it all approved and integrated as part of ongoing process, a programme? Do you really think that rogue state isn't trying to get into places in the times when Donald Trump hasn't tweeted something? Shouldn't you have a programme that aims to keep them out *all* the time? Are you aware that a critical patch gets deployed the same way as any other patch? Why all the fuss?

Oh, "there are differences", I hear you say. You're now going to lecture me about them. Very well. Why were you able to lecture me on that, but not create an operational process that considered the same differences you just lectured me about? Ahh...

Your end-state should be to have all this defined, so that you walk into the office the morning after the next massive super scary vulnerability is announced, and at most ask someone on the team:

"Hey did we..."
"The Citrix one?"
"Yeah.
"Yup, tested then done."
"Sweet, gonna go back downstairs and grab a salted caramel muffin."

CISOs burning out after 17-18 months? Really?

I love solving problems. This is not a stressful job when you solve them properly. It's fun and rewarding.

The last item I see many CISOs spend a ton of time on?

Vendors.

Good lord. If some CISOs spent half as much time talking to their own business as they do to vendors they'd probably discover enough to be able to reduce the business' risk exposure by 90%.

What I find particularly interesting is just how much many CISO are actually influenced or flat-out led by the vendors, or various industry publications (many of which are backed by or written by vendors).

Conversely, a CISO knowing exactly what he/she wants to address a specific issue around protecting a specific business area or function, is a rarity.

When an outside vendor is leading your security strategy more than your own business is, something is wrong.

I use "strategy" loosely here as I've heard CISOs, when asked what their strategy was respond with "We're going to roll out Darktrace."

Just *no*. That is not a strategy.

You know what I rarely if ever see CISOs discuss in these forums?

Engagement. And I don't mean asking for more toys or money or staff. I mean actually interacting with people to find out more about how they work and how security can help them do that and help them do it securely. HR, Marketing, Sales, Engineering, Customer Support, the exec team, Legal... Go talk to them!

Once you've done that you can actually improve IT and business process.

You know, to rectify the things that cause the issues for which you *think* you need all that staff and tooling to deal with. To keep them from happening in the first place.

Nope. I never hear that topic come up. Certainly not in a holistically thought, prescriptive, and sustainable way.

Instead it's endless chatter about risk management metrics, firefighting, and having vendors tell them how they can fix "their pain".

So yeah. Don't be a "CISO." At least not that kind of CISO.

Negative Information Security Culture

Few things irk me more than seeing security people badmouth others. I've lost count of the number of times I see 2 or more security professionals in a room start mocking people about how stupid and ignorant they are about security. Ironically demonstrating that *they*, the security professionals, are the ones lacking the skills to push security across an organisation. An organisation made up of people.

I find there is an alarming amount of negativity and blame culture within Information Security. Towards senior management (C-level & the board), towards IT, and towards end-users.

The users in particular are often a target, and I've lost count of the number of times I've seen security people blame them.

Here's the user scenario:

Bob from marketing clicked on a phishing email, systems got compromised, the situation quickly escalated. Bob caused a massive breach, potentially costing tens of millions or more.

But now let's go into a little more detail:

Bob *from marketing* clicks on a phishing email, which wasn't filtered. The attacker then manages to compromise the laptop undetected due to no one ever having bothered to configure the endpoint protection solution properly, the attacker then escalates their privilege to admin because of a poorly secured image (or because Bob was given local admin rights because his laptop build didn't allow him to do his job), the attacker manages to install tools undetected, stealthily scan your network evading poorly thought out network controls, break into your misconfigured gateway, compromise your routers due to default passwords or old firmware, access vulnerable services through misconfigured firewalls, hop from segment to segment in your datacentre (premise or cloud, it doesn't matter) through the various unpatched vulnerabilities on your servers which the attacker can then use to tunnel over any ports they desire, install command and control infrastructure, locate and download millions of data records, potentially wipe out the entire infrastructure (a problem since the backups haven't been kept offline or tested) and anything else they please.

Are we really going to say this was Bob's fault? When we not only failed to protect him and train him properly on the phishing email, but failed every single step of the way along the attacker's path or "kill chain" that allowed them to completely compromise our environment?

I'm going to give a nod to Matthew Trump here and his work around the phenomenon of "human error."

In a nutshell, it's essentially a meaningless label. It should never be considered a root cause in any kind of investigation. If a user did something there was likely a reason for it. Was the user trained? Was something mislabelled? Could something have been mistaken for something else? Was stress mixed into a situation that could have led to confusion? Was there anything informing the user he/she was doing something questionable? Or a control that would have stopped the user from being able to complete an action that shouldn't have been taken?

More mature industries such as construction, healthcare, aerospace, and oil & gas have something in common: They do not accept "user error" as a root cause determination. This forces them to usually make changes to the user's environment to make sure things don't happen again. If a pilot confused a critical alarm with an innocuous one because they sounded the same, the sound of the alarm is changed. If a nurse grabbed the wrong medication because of poor labelling, the labelling system is changed.

Always ask what more you can do to help the user rather than to blame the user.

Remember, security is usually a non-functional role, we do not typically produce revenue. Those users are doing the actual work that is paying our salaries, we work for them, to protect them, and to enable them to continue doing that important work.

Then there's the blame of IT and management. I'll only cover a couple of things here as we'll explore these topics in more detail later.

IT is functional. Be aware of the functional work being done, work we're not qualified to do. Respect it, understand their priorities, and know what management pressures and metrics they work under.

Then there's management. Lack of support, lack of resource, "They don't understand risk!" and all that.

Let's be clear about something: C-level management do understand business risk, probably better than us.

What they don't understand is us, and part of that is because we don't understand them or the business so we're not speaking or approaching in a relevant way.

We can fix this by working on ourselves instead of blaming.

More on this later.

Culture as a Root Cause

We just discussed blaming users as the root cause of a particular problem. Now, let's look at organisational culture as a root cause. And just to be clear, I'm talking about the culture *within* the InfoSec organisation.

As I'm writing this, the Boeing 737 MAX debacle has been in the news.

The 737 MAX issues have a huge number of technical reasons; from poor design of the electronic anti-stall system (MCAS), in turn only really needed because the aircraft had to make physical/engineering compromises with its oversized engines, now so big that they can't fit under the existing wings and therefore had to be mounted much further forward than is ideal and shifting the plane's balance which makes it prone to stalling.

Why this awkwardly compromised design? To avoid the certification and training costs that would be associated with a "new" design which would have been suitable for the new power-plants, which in turn could have hampered sales as airlines would have had to recertify its pilots on a new (no longer a 737) model. These savings make the 737 MAX attractive to airlines and allow for a faster rollout.

The thing is this aircraft has significantly different dynamics than a regular 737. Heck, an Airbus 320 possibly flies more like a regular 737 then a 737 MAX does because of the extreme engineering compromises present in the MAX caused by trying to keep the 737 designation for those financial reasons.

Then there's the debacle of removing procedures from flight manuals as to "not confuse" pilots, general poor engineering, quality control issues in Boeing's plants, conflicts with self-certification rather than the FAA performing independent verification, and more.

But the overwhelming headline about the Boeing 737 MAX story isn't one of engineering or technical gaffes.

The headlines point the finger directly at the *leadership* and their culture.

As they should.

And yet, I can't recall ever seeing leadership publicly held to account for *our* plane crashes: the big breaches that happen on Information Security's watch.

I already know, from the level of indoctrination and the mentality that seems so prevalent in our industry, that many people reading the above paragraph are thinking of the CEOs and other CxO's not giving the CISOs of the world enough attention, resource, and authority. But no, I am pointing the finger straight at the CISO. It's time to stop blaming and take responsibility.

"But, but but…!"

No. There are no excuses, only challenges. Difficulty is not an acceptable reason for not trying, for not doing our best.

Based on the fact that the vast majority of large breaches are caused by simple and usually easily fixable oversights, we are doing far from our best in terms of delivering value and assurance to our organisations.

It's time to hold ourselves accountable.

When one of the top recommendations I give people is to *zero* the InfoSec budget for 6 months so that they're forced to look at what *free* actions they can take (because they tend to have a better likelihood to find the kinds of issues that cause most of the breaches we see making headlines), it's apparent that we can do a lot better.

When I go into a client site, the security leadership is the first thing I look at. When I see a lack of attention to detail, care, altruism, engagement with or knowledge of the business, I know I'm going to find significant technical issues as a result. Issues most wouldn't consider connected or related, but they very much are.

Also telling is the amount of resistance I get when presenting these things to the security community. I've been pulled off of assignments, had consulting engagements terminated, and even been fired by the security leadership for finding security issues.

Lawyers, DPOs, and non-security executives typically make up less than 2% of the attendees at security events. Yet, when I present about my services to find issues others have missed, they represent the vast majority of the people that contact me, and the only ones that ever want a proposal.

The odd Information Security practitioner that does contact me tends to be younger, in a non-management position, who found the insights refreshing. The Security decision-makers on the other hand are rarely appreciative of new ideas.

Too few people within security leadership roles want to do the right thing, to put people and the whole organisation first.

Aside: To see what positive ethical leadership can do, check out the story around Southwest Airlines in Dr Mansur Hasib's must-read book, *Information Security Leadership*.

The People Reality

People. Process. Technology.

In that order.

We often mention these 3 things as the 3 aspects of Information Security. But much of the Information Security I've seen in practice has done these things backwards and halfway.

People, which I feel you could also replace with "the business", is where the work happens. The ensemble of human beings working towards the organisation's goals.

We must understand this goal and work out how we can enable, support, and protect it.

That should be done by establishing business and, consequently, IT processes which support those objectives.

It is only at this stage that technology comes in, as the tools to enable the efficient delivery of those processes.

It has to be said that sometimes certain tools can also provide the visibility needed to identify where processes can be improved, resulting in an avenue for continuous improvement of the processes they support. But we have to remember that ultimately the tools support the processes which in turn support the business/people.

In summary: *People* working on a business goal, through the use of effective *processes* allowing efficiency, security, and integrity, in turn supported by *technology*.

The reality is all too often something different. As I said, we seem to do it backwards and halfway:

We focus primarily on technology. Tools, tools, tools, dictated by the latest trends and a highly commercialised security industry. These tools do address real issues, but they address them reactively, and the issues themselves only exist (or only exist on such a large scale) because we've failed to align ourselves with the people (business) and therefore so have our processes.

Processes which then cannot be effective because we're basing them around how to apply the technology without an understanding of how the business works. If we're following them (the processes) at all.

Let's be honest, InfoSec processes are often little more than tick-box exercises. They're not made with the business in mind and rarely address how integrity and consistency of the business processes should be ensured long-term. To make matters worse, as poor as they are, they're often not even followed, end up left in a drawer, and we struggle to find them at audit time when we need to update them to make it *look* like we use them. Again, because they serve primarily as a tick-box exercise, and not as a way of implementing holistically thought-out processes to the benefit of the business in a consistent and ongoing way.

We now get to the people bit… Which we often omit to do altogether. I've lost count of the number of times I walked into a business and after 3 days there knew more about the company and what mattered to it staying in business than heads of IT and Information Security that had been there for half a decade or more.

Yes indeed. All too often "People, process, technology" is actually:

"Technology, half-assed process to tick the box, and no clue what the people/business even does."

We have to make security about the business and its people, rather than our beloved technology, or we will never be successful at neither securing nor helping the business.

Communication

I often find myself talking to senior people that are not in the InfoSec sphere such as COOs, CFOs, CEOs, trying to explain things about Information Security to them. Their default stance is one that many security professionals will find all too familiar: They do not listen.

But that stance only lasts for about 30 seconds once I give them an analogy they can relate to and tell them a story they don't expect: That security isn't that complicated if you break it down, and that a lot of what they've been hearing about is bogus. I also express concern about what they want to achieve, not just "security" for security's sake

After that, they are often captivated. Why? Because I am speaking plain English, explaining concepts that they, as business people and leaders, not only understand, but are quite familiar with. Plus, they feel good about taking the technocrats down a peg!

All of a sudden, they understand what is being said and it's a revelation to them. They feel you've given them some grasp or control over security, for the first time.

Why was their initial reaction, for those first 30 seconds, to tune me out? Because of how people have always been approaching them about security, how it has always been explained to them, and sold to them: Through complicated technical terms they could not possibly be expected to understand, and through fear-based marketing. And the simple fact that most of the InfoSec industry lives in a reactive bubble that doesn't address the common-sense realities of the real world, which makes it all the harder to understand to the layman.

Management nowadays know that cyber security is a thing, that there is a real threat, but they do not understand what exactly it means or what they should be doing about it. But they are not experts, so they need to trust others to take care of it for them. How can they develop trust in us when they can't understand what we're talking about?

I have lost count of how many times I've heard CxO's tell me things such as:

"In 10 years no one has ever explained it to me this way."

"I can't recall ever having such an enjoyable conversation with a security person!"

"You're the first one that's made this make sense to us!"

"Interesting approach. I actually get it... And I like it!"

The above is often said with big smiles because we're just so excited that we're communicating and understanding each other. As human beings we are wired to get exciting about being able to communicate.

But the fact that they are getting so excited because it's the first time that someone has ever explained things to them in way they could understand is also a damning indictment of our long-standing failure to communicate as Information Security professionals.

It gets worse because this lack of engagement, of communication, is not limited to the C-level, it extends to our relationships with IT heads, other department heads, end users, *everyone*.

It is a core contributor to why today's Information Security status quo is a hopeless, disengaged, and expensive reactive affair.

It is, more often than not, why we fail.

Engaging the Business

There is a statement sometimes made that it's not possible to know how to secure a business if we don't know what matters most to it, what areas have the biggest contribution, how they would be impacted by certain events, and so on.

This is all absolutely true, and yet most of us rarely step out of the security department and into IT operations, let alone into the wider parts of the business.

But I would argue there are even more important reasons for doing so than the ones listed above.

If we explore the business, we are given a tremendous opportunity to show our faces. The default assumption of many people is that security people get in the way, and it's extremely difficult to dispel this over email, no matter how good your intentions are.

It allows us to be seen as human beings, as people that actually care (caveat: you have to actually care), and as potential contributors and enablers.

I like to go out of my way to show that I want to understand their work and their needs, to show concern for their work getting done, and for its integrity, availability, and confidentiality.

When they see you putting effort in doing all this for them, in such a way that considers their needs and doesn't cause interference, you stop having security be the last people they want to speak with. Sometimes you even become their favourite team to work with.

This means that when anything changes in their environment, they'll ask you about whether it's ok. When they realise something may be off, they won't hesitate to tell you, even if they were at fault.

They feel comfortable sharing and confessing things to you, they sympathise with security more, they become more conscious about it, and they even become your eyes and ears to what they see around them,

I often find that, aside from the security solutions/processes/aspects, the IT facilities provisioned often aren't ideal, especially in fast moving/changing environments such as R&D. Each time I get a request for a security exemption or anything else from a team or department I haven't dealt with yet, I take that opportunity to meet the stakeholders face to face, find out how they work, and why they're requesting certain things.

It's often because they've been provisioned something that isn't ideal. I then take it on myself to get IT to change the way they provision that team, solving the issue and many more, and also developing a great relationship and perception as someone truly there to help.

All this leads me to discover things I could not have discovered through org charts, asset management and more.

You may have been spending millions on all kinds of security tooling, but did you know a small subset of department X has 17 million customer records on a USB stick because they use it as part of a manual process involving some arcane system that doesn't show up in your asset management, representing a far greater risk to the organisation than any of the things you're currently spending millions on managing and mitigating?

Well now you do, because you actually went to talk to people while building a climate of trust that you were there to help and that they could tell you anything.

Bonus points: Building that positive helpful and engaging reputation will go a long way in helping you get that executive traction later.

Board Games

Speaking of executive traction...

There is a picture that seems to make a recurring appearance on my LinkedIn feed.

It shows a bunch of people in suits at a big table, and a bunch of children and a man in a suit at a little kids' table in the foreground. The man at the kids' table has a tag that says "CISO", and a man from the big table, with the tag "Board of Directors", comes down to invite the CISO to their table.

Whenever this picture comes up I see hundreds of security people comment in agreement. They all believe they're not in the right place, that they should be on the board to have the influence to get things done, squash resistance, and get the needed funding.

I hate that picture.

Firstly, that's not what being on the board is about and that kind of thinking is the reason those people aren't on the board to begin with. I strongly believe good executives and board members are those that care about the organisation, the business, the people. It's about making things work together as a whole. They don't blame.

Secondly (and even more importantly for this coming part), they're not trying to do a damn thing to get to where they claim they need to be, preferring instead to moan and [subconsciously perhaps] have the excuse for their own lack of effectiveness that they weren't high up enough to fix things.

Here's the thing. Influencing isn't about being on or reporting to the board. Driving widespread change can be made easier by being there, sure, but if you can't get the board to listen to you, how are you going to get on there?

What is stopping you from speaking to a random person in a hallway, café, or grocery store?

Nothing, right?

What is stopping you from speaking to your CFO, COO, or CEO? Same answer.

You're not on the board? How is that even relevant?

There is nothing stopping you from engaging these people as human beings outside of that boardroom.

A good 1-minute pitch to the CEO in the hallway of after they finish an address can set you up for 15 minutes over a coffee, which can get you a 30-minute meeting (perhaps with the COO or chair of the board this time), and you can start building a trusted relationship with them. Alternatively take the time to create a *quality* report of the right length, detail, and tone and circulate it.

I've had a role where the I reported up to a CIO who filtered out all my security concerns to the board. He would report back to me that there was no interest in, or budget for, security due to "strategic priorities." It would turn out he was, unbeknownst to me, actually spending the board-allocated security budget, which did exist, on personal projects.

Even unaware of the second part, this was obviously a problem and completely undermined even the possibility of having a security programme, let alone an effective one. What was I to do? Complain about it?

I ended up catching the CEO as she left a meeting. Complimented her on a couple of things mentioned in some recent internal announcements, mentioned some of my contributions (if you keep engaging and contributing everywhere you can you will have some ammunition here), and offered a coffee to discuss further. 3 weeks later we're discussing Porsche models one-on-one in the executive offices and working on setting up regular board-level security briefings.

It only takes initiative and engagement. One caveat is you must become someone worth listening to. More on this later book number 2 of this series (*Influencing InfoSec*), but for now just know that you need to demonstrate that:

- You understand the business;

- You speak in business terms (or plain English) and provide value;
- You care for the business and others;
- You have a clear strategic vision;
- You have the ability and drive to engage;
- You have a solid personal brand.

These will get you listened to. That's it for now.

Reputation

If we're to have influence and traction, or have success in building it up, our reputation inside the organisation is important.

My 2 favourite quotes about reputation are as follows:

It takes 20 years to build a reputation and five minutes to ruin it. If you think about that, you'll do things differently. – Warren Buffet

And…

It takes many good deeds to build a good reputation, and only one bad one to lose it. – Benjamin Franklin

Both are very similar, but with one slight difference. The first focuses on time, the second on the number of deeds, and what I believe that says is that we can shorten the former by stepping up the latter, but time will always be a factor. This is one more reason why a long-term strategic approach is necessary – we must realise we can't change things immediately because it will take time to build up the needed influence – but it also means we need to get started on that strategic approach as soon as possible.

We have to be aware that as much as we think InfoSec may be great and important, our general reputation is awful. The perception of security is nearly always negative due to the poor approach and engagement that's been taken by many in the industry for decades.

It's so bad that when I introduce myself as Information Security to people in most organisations, probably a third of those people physically recoil, and most of the rest become guarded (the more perceptive you become the more you'll realise this happens).

We're starting on the back foot, and it's important to immediately and consistently respond to this kind of reaction with reassurance that we do *not* want to be blockers. Communicate that we have a different approach, we rather enable, take security-relevant work off of their shoulders, that we understand they play important functional roles we couldn't hope to do ourselves, that we want to help and complement rather than police, etc. We do this with words, but we must also back it up with action as much as possible.

I often advocate that we have to go to others, do the work ourselves, even when a lot of it isn't officially our job.

I use the analogy of the "2-way street". Normally this expression means we have to go and meet people in the middle. But security is a different animal where it's important to get ahead of things and we must therefore often go all the way to the other end.

"But that's not fair! They should come to us too!"

Tough. Suck it up and do it.

Firstly, as mentioned before, our reputation is historically terrible. No one wants to come to us, for good reason. We have to go to them in order to repair that reputation.

Secondly, however much extra effort this will cost, it's a drop in the bucket compared to the endless amount of frustrating and unrewarding reactive security work we'll have to do if we don't go all the way to them, repair our reputation, and proactively drive change.

It may not be "our job" according to your role or job description, but it will make it a lot easier.

Much more importantly than that, it will deliver better results, assurance, cost savings to the business (because you'll be spending less!), because it allows *us* to work *with* people, to find out what is truly happening, and empowering us to deliver real high-value change that is also personally *rewarding**.

*Just think of the huge mental health benefits for security practitioners here.

Downstream Engagement

Engagement is quite possibly the single most powerful force in scaling information security throughout an organisation. It's the most important thing you can do. But why?

Well, not only are most large breaches caused by a lack of awareness of the organisation, but a huge amount of operational Information Security work done today in most organisations could be eliminated by addressing certain things further upstream before they multiply into a myriad of issues requiring security controls. But how do we do that?

Instead of being reactive, we have to be proactive. But that requires influence in things that are often beyond our authority or control and we need to influence people that do not report to us, and in some cases may be higher up the totem pole than us.

In order for people in other areas of the business (who have different objectives and priorities) to do things for us outside of their core job role, we must build emotional and psychological involvement.

We cannot just expect people to do things because we want them to. We ourselves wouldn't react positively towards strangers that just came up to us expecting things and helping themselves to our time and effort.

The first thing I do when I need to approach a new group of people over which I have no control* is go out of my way to help them, in any way. It doesn't have to be work related. It can literally be offering the whole room to help them move, mow the lawn, fix their chainsaw, change their oil, anything! Most will laugh but take the offer positively. Some will actually take you up on it. Follow through, it is a tremendous opportunity and will gain the respect not just of that individual, but of their whole circle. That respect and recognition will pay enormous dividends over the long term

*I'll also do this pre-emptively to build relationships and support long before I need anything from them. This will often result in them fortifying your position by spreading a favourable opinion of you throughout their peers

But it's surely impossible to have this level of interaction with everyone in an organization, what if there are 10,000 or more people? Firstly, the most important thing is to try anyway, always. Secondly, you won't actually have to engage everyone *directly*. Few things are as scalable and contagious as human influence.

Let me give you some examples of three different types of downward influence. I'll call them *direct*, *indirect*, and *"herd"* influence.

I once started a role managing Information Security for a large account. After a few weeks, a special case around one of the employees working in the call centre on a different floor of the building was brought to my attention.

This person, Khalid, had a degenerative disease that affected his hearing (among many other things). He could not fit his headphones over his hearing aids and struggled to hear without them in. He had a device that could connect directly to the phone and send audio to his hearing aids, but it used Bluetooth, which was a policy violation.

In a textbook example of bad bureaucracy, whether to allow him to violate policy had apparently been under discussion between HR, InfoSec, and Legal for 9 months. There had been nearly 60 (!) emails exchanged in that time with no decisive action taken.

There were concerns about security, about being sued over not making reasonable adjustments for the disability, and of simply having Khalid do his job.

My first question was how the hearing device worked. No one knew.

I asked his supervisor if he could have Khalid bring in the hearing aids' Bluetooth phone adapter (for lack of a better term) device the next day in order to give me a quick show and tell.

After meeting him it seemed to me that the security risk was extremely limited. While Khalid regularly dealt with payment details over the phone, so did everyone else around him and they could have stolen them in half a dozen different ways if they'd wanted to. Khalid worked on the 4th floor, the building was an old mill and had 2-foot-thick stone walls, and there were no other structures nearby. The odds of that Bluetooth signal leaking out were pretty much nil.

We had a friendly 10-minute chat, and I told him to just start using the device and I would put in a policy exception for him right away.

This tiny simple act cemented a positive relationship between security (me) with Khalid. That is direct influence that will ease any eventual future interaction with him.

But my helping him was also witnessed by the people on the floor who saw me coming in and taking the time to sort out their colleague's issue, with which they'd seen him struggle for 9 months, and created a positive impression even though I'd not helped *them*. This impression was then associated with the broader security team and materials. That is indirect influence.

The result? Despite there being no new awareness campaigns or security communications of any kind, the number of GDPR and clean desk incidents dropped by nearly a third the following month.

Then there is herd influence, or perhaps the herd "effect" is a better term. Quite simply, people will tend to treat you as others around them treat you, even if they don't know why. Here's a perfect example:

About a year ago I went to the grocery store and bought £7.15 worth of dog food. I held up my card to pay contactless, heard the beep, felt my phone buzz in my pocket with the notification, and walked off to my car.

I got home and saw the following on my phone screen: Sainsbury's - £7.15 - Payment DECLINED. Oops.

I thought I had misplaced my card that morning and blocked it in the app. I thought I had unblocked it, but it seems I didn't do so successfully. The beeps and buzzes were warning me of a payment failure, not success.

I went back the next morning, explained the situation and asked how I could pay the £7.15 to the stunned disbelief of 5 employees and a dozen or more shoppers overhearing the conversation. Many looked at me wondering what was wrong with me, but the interaction would not be forgotten.

It was so unprecedented that I had to take cash out because no one could figure out how to charge me electronically for something done the day before. I left them the money and they'd sort it out.

I paid £7.15 (which I owed anyway) and ended up being the talk of the store among the staff, who now recognise me, hold me in high regard, and will be happy to help me in the future because they know I'm not in it for just me.

A few days later I popped into the same grocery store to buy more dog food (he eats a lot). While I was there I picked up a belt. I went through the self-checkout (and managed to pay successfully this time), walked the 50 or so yards from the checkout to the door and, just as I exited, the alarm went off. Presumably from the tag on the belt.

Two employees ran up to check my purchase but stopped after just a few paces. Still standing 40 yards away they said:

"Oh, it's you!"

They wave me off with a smile and head back to work. The trust has been established. They didn't feel the need to check anything. After all this is the guy who turns himself in when he accidentally takes something.

The interesting thing here is that only one of the two employees actually knew who I was from the last incident, the second one merely followed his lead. His colleague treated me a certain way, therefore so did he, without even knowing why. This is yet another way influence can be massively scaled up.

When I helped Khalid, I spent 20 minutes helping one person, it was seen by maybe 10 people directly, who would then smile and wave or say hello when I walked through their floor. After another month, with no real additional effort on my part, the number of people that smiled and waved at me on that floor was at least 30, because they saw how the person next to them reacted to me, and it spread. Their willingness to accept what I asked of them, their receptiveness to *my* needs, also heightened, without me ever having done anything for them. (I would be happy to help if ever they asked me for something – we have to live up to the impression of ourselves that we've created.)

Please note that I am talking about engagement with end users, not senior people. I think this is important because while you should engage with *everyone* in this same way, many that do practice engagement only do so upstream and see themselves as "above" others in less senior positions. If we care about people and the organisation, we have to engage in all directions.

I once had an interview at a large shipping company. Their Head of IT told me about their frustration with their warehouse staff whom they couldn't get to abide by GDPR and other data protection policies. They were constantly leaving shipping manifests and other data laying around.

On my way out, I got a little lost (inner and outer warehouse perimeters, lots of fences, etc.) and ended up asking a warehouse worker for directions and striking up a conversation. I spoke to Gavin for 5 minutes.

He was a ball of pure enthusiasm. He told me about his job, how much he loved it, about his colleagues, how one is now his wife, his kids (he ended up offering me a lift to my car and there was a child seat in his), and all kinds of stuff. He was just a really nice, friendly, helpful guy. The kind of person that puts a smile on your face.

He dropped me off at my car and, as I stepped out, I asked him a question:

"Gavin, who can you name from the IT team here?"

No one.

The IT and InfoSec office overlooked the warehouse. You walked through the warehouse to reach the cafeteria.

Gavin had been there for 7 years.

The interview feedback? The Head of IT I spoke with wrote the recruiter back saying, in all caps, that I was "EXACTLY WHAT WE NEED!" referring to the engaging approach I had presented during the interview.

I followed up a few weeks later to find that the company's [award-winning] CIO ended up outsourcing all of its security to an MSP instead.

Zero knowledge of the business, zero engagement.

Growth

I start some of my talks with the following story. It's worth sharing.

A couple of years ago, I was contacted on LinkedIn by a man named Peter.

Peter wasn't in information security nor was he extremely technical. What Peter did, among some other projects, was run something called Director School. In short, he helped educate company directors.

Some of this was actually technology training, but at a very basic level. We have to realise many executives are well in their 60s and some struggle with today's technology. Basic things like apps, using an Android device or iPhone, and understanding how computers network together can all be quite a challenge for this demographic. This is what Peter was working on when he contacted me.

He wanted to expand the scope of his offering to include some information security coverage and thought I was saying some interesting things about the topic. I was presenting a much simpler way of dealing with issues and doing so in plain English rather than all the industry terminology and intimidating technobabble.

He asked me to meet him for a coffee. I accepted. (Top tip: people tend to do that, accept going for coffee.)

We met in a hotel lobby and he asked me to tell him my story because there was something different here.

I started talking, and talking, and kept talking... It was a shameful (shameless?) 30-minute monologue, only interrupted by the occasional compliment or complimentary question by Peter who listened with great attention and interest, saying nice things to me.

Needless to say, it was a very pleasant "conversation", very flattering, a nice little ego boost. It felt great to be recognised as this was also a particularly difficult time for me, in the middle of a 9-month unemployment stint due to being "too big" for roles with no end in sight. A good time.

Then he had to pop into the restroom, pausing halfway there to throw me yet one more compliment.

A few minutes later he came back, stopped by the bar for 2 more coffees, put them down on our table, sat down, looked at me with a smile, and said:

"Here's the thing..."

He then proceeded, for the next 20 minutes, unabashed, without pause, to, and there's no other way of saying this, rip me a new one.

He went over everything I said, pointing out ways I could have done things better, what I did wrong, etc.

My good feeling went away. It was replaced by a very unpleasant feeling, an uncomfortable one.

Many of the examples he threw back at me involved how I could have handled things differently. The thing is, I had actually tried most of the alternatives he was suggesting, and part of me desperately wanted to say that, to defend myself. But he didn't even give me the chance to do so, and in my mind I was falling behind and starting to stockpile corrections, and maybe excuses.

Sure, I did try that, but did I try hard enough? Could I have done it better? The doubts started coming.

Then there was the 10% of things he was saying where he was genuinely and completely right. Here too my first instinct was to say "Argh! I was right 90% of the time!" and make excuses for that other 10%.

But Peter wasn't attacking me. He was challenging me. He had my best interests in mind. And I let go.

This took the edge off the sting of what he was saying, and I started focusing more on what I could learn from it. I came to regard that uncomfortable feeling as growth.

Sure, we all grow all the time (hopefully), but that's usually in tiny increments, and on the path we're already on. It's not uncomfortable growth.

The uncomfortable kind, the growth that gives you broad new ideas, that makes you reflect and question yourself, now that's orders of magnitudes more powerful.

We have to realise we may be wrong, no matter how many people agree with us, we have to question, and we have to accept to occasionally feel like an idiot in front of others.

Good people will not hold that against us. And if we're dealing with people that do, then "so what?" We'll have looked a fool to one closed-minded person and be wiser in front of every other person we'll meet for the rest of our lives for it. It's a small price to pay. Heck, it's a bargain. You should smile inside at the thought that a piece of growth, which will empower you for the rest of your life, came at the meaningless cost of some cocky person's ego.

Embrace every challenge as an opportunity to question yourself. It may confirm your thinking, it may cast it into doubt. Never be afraid to explore the latter.

Sometimes I'm wrong, sometimes I'm even generally right but wrong due to a particular scenario. This is one reason why I like to look at things on a case by case basis and why I implore you to take much of what I say as ideas and generalisations and to reach your own final conclusions in whatever situation you find yourself in.

The more often I *admit* to being wrong, even if just to myself, the more often I'll be right in the future.

Sometimes we'll get "attacked" by difficult people on something where we know to be right*, and there's nothing to learn from the discussion. But even here we can reflect and learn on how to better deal with such people and situations. Something that will come in very useful indeed when managing difficult individuals, sometimes in important positions, in the future.

By the way, when you are experiencing this kind of negative behaviour, be ready to walk away. Your time and wellbeing are valuable, don't let them take it away from you.

*Just be damn sure to keep an open mind though!

Failing

I once posted something on LinkedIn about being rejected for a role because I didn't anticipate the need to go in depth about my technical knowledge, assuming it was implied through my experience, CV, and several more general statements. It was ironic because I'm one of the most technical strategic-level people I know and regularly talking about how people need to get broader and deeper understanding of how stuff works, even those in management, to avoid disconnects that lead to dangerous security errors and gaps.

I got a lot of replies along the line that it was their loss, that they should have asked if it was so critical, and that they should have followed up. But ultimately it was entirely my failure. Which brings me to failure.

When we set out to do something and we don't succeed, we have failed. It's that simple.

The fact that some equipment didn't work, or something unanticipated happened, or that we did our job perfectly but someone else didn't doesn't matter. We failed. It's the result that matters. Had we truly wanted to succeed, in hindsight, we could have better checked the equipment, we could have anticipated more, we could even have gone and done the other people's jobs for them to make sure they were done right, or guided them to do it better themselves. But we didn't, and as a result, we failed.

Forget the stigma around failure. Failing in this way can be acceptable. And there is no greater tool for personal growth than failing and working out why, so it doesn't happen again.

Airplanes today are safer because of a rigorous doctrine of root cause analysis and rectification. The root causes are never "human error", investigators always go the extra mile to see how the human's error happened in the first place, how it could have been prevented and how to address that.

I've talked about blame culture before. "The user messed up" or "Management wouldn't give us the resources" are the kinds of things I hear often and detest. It is a 2-way street and you have to meet the other party. We cannot excuse our not doing everything we could have because others didn't come to us, or even half way. Sometimes we have to go all the way down the street and meet them on the other end. It's not about what our job is. It's about what we can do.

About 10 years ago I was continuously disappointed by people's performance and kept having to do their jobs for them to make sure it was right. It was, in a word, annoying. It was also exhausting and unsustainable.

It took me a further few years to start focusing less on doing other people's jobs and instead start working out why they weren't doing them properly themselves. Was it motivation, care, engagement? Maybe a lack of skill, or the fact that they didn't know how the pieces fit together? Missing curiosity perhaps?

First, I thought I had learned to accept a compromise in the quality of work, meaning I could allow myself to delegate, but then I got more involved in the people themselves.

I don't know what our society, our educational system, our work environments, and our industry are doing to people, but I am nothing short of staggered at how good we are at eliminating curiosity, critical thinking, holistic thinking, and the belief of our own potential. Most people don't have one tenth of the breadth and/or depth of knowledge that they could easily have. We could complain about it and blame them for it, which is what we usually do (as I did – guilty as charged), or we could go and inspire them, mentor them, teach them. The beauty of it is that you don't have to actually teach them the other nine tenths they should be capable of. You just have to make them hungry to learn.

I believe, despite all signs to the contrary, that this hunger to learn is in our nature, and that it can usually be awoken no matter how hard we've tried to kill it off.

All of a sudden, you're not dealing with a bunch of annoying slackers anymore, you're dealing with brilliant minds, overtaking even their mentors in certain areas. They learn not just skills, but character traits like curiosity, dependability, thoroughness, communication and human engagement skills. They're no longer a burden, they're a team of superstars, and 5 of them will do what 50 drones couldn't hope to.

Comfort Zone

Growth is important, more important than just traditional learning. But, as we mentioned earlier, real growth takes us to new places and tends to be uncomfortable.

The more we think we know, the more we are experts in the status quo and how things are "supposed" to be done, the more we have built a vast foundation of knowledge and experience in an area, the more emotionally invested we become, the more we are actually prone to resisting change.

Emotional investment can be a powerful force, and it can be a negative one when it comes to resisting change.

That's right. It's not the newbies lacking experience that are uncomfortable with change. Well, ok, they are, but nowhere near as much as those with entrenched knowledge and experience. The tricky part is that the entrenched ones also find it harder to see it, to even realise it. Trust me, I know, I've been there.

This is one of the reasons I love working with fresh talent so much. While everyone dismisses them as being too inexperienced (some even attack me, calling me irresponsible and saying I'm putting my organisation at risk by hiring them), the mere fact that they're not stuck in a certain way of thinking (the parking lot way) is a huge, and I mean *huge* enabler.

But first I want to run you through the contents of a slide I sometimes show at my talks. It's a look at the situation we face today. It is, as Information Security professionals, the world we live in for the last couple decades.

It is our pain.

So, let's look at our *pain*.

- Growing security costs.
- Increasing pressures/workloads.
- Spiralling complexity.
- An ever-increasing number of breaches.
- The realisation that it isn't a matter of if we're going to suffer a breach, but of when.
- A shortage of over 4,000,000 workers in the industry.
- And top it all off with increasing overhead from regulation.

Is it any wonder we are under stress, and that our jobs are all but impossible to perform as expected by senior management and the public?

There's just one thing… I'm not terribly sure whether this is really our pain or not. It depends how you look at it (much room for interpretation here). I feel much of this is self-inflicted. There is one thing that I am certain of though:

Whether or not it's really our pain, it has absolutely become our *comfort zone*.

These are the things we like to say to get our way, to gain sympathy, to waive responsibility, and far too often to not act, or be allowed to act in such a way that failure is an option, because it's understandable, because poor us, look at what we have to deal with.

We may be working ourselves to death without a chance of succeeding, certainly not to the levels I feel we should be, but we do so willingly.

I try to get people to see things from a more proactive standpoint, where we give up on how we've been doing things, accept that what we've been doing isn't working and approach things differently. A way that I've shown works and works well, with far less cost and effort.

The resistance is staggering.

Much like an abused animal that's spent a miserable life in a cage, when you open the door it doesn't want to come out. Instead it hides in the deepest corner of that cage. That cage, despite all the misery, is where it feels most comfortable.

We fear the unknown, despite all of its great possibilities, more than the hell we know.

It means sacrificing ideas we may have held as truths and walking away from a potentially significant amount of invested time and effort. It means possibly giving up some of our importance.

But to regain our objectivity, we have to.

The good news is it allows us to find a better way, and to make the right choices.

The War on Terror

Remember that the fundamental goal of Information Security in most organisations has nothing to do with computers. It is about protecting the business from damages, typically financial, direct and otherwise.

We have to break it down to this level to understand that when we are spending more resource than is necessary we are not preventing losses, we are *incurring* losses.

From a business perspective we are having the same negative impact as the thing we're supposed to be fighting.

Let's take a little detour.

At the time of writing, the United States has spent over six trillion dollars ($6,000,000,000,000) fighting "the war on terror." And yet, this war on extremism has only caused more extremism, resulting in an endless and ever-growing cycle.

This is not dissimilar to the way we currently do Information Security. While we're not actively making cybercrime grow, we're failing to resolve it, and incentivising its growth through our failures; If systems were better secured making it unlikely to ever be able to break in, far fewer people would get into the cybercrime game, just as far more people would get into bank robbery if we left their security with as many gaps in coverage as we do in cyberspace.

That same six trillion dollars would have been more than enough to give a free college education to everyone in the United States, which would arguably have resulted in a boost to the GDP of more than that amount, while vastly improving people's lives by a margin far superior than by how much it was disrupted or made worse by occasional terrorism, even as bad as 9/11 was (which, by the way, we failed to prevent regardless of anti-terror spending).

Interestingly, you would have had enough left over from that 6 trillion dollars to also pay for a college education for every person living in Iraq, Iran, Afghanistan, Syria, Yemen, and more. Leading to the improvement of further millions of lives, gaining their gratitude ("hearts and minds") and dramatically reducing extremism. (Just like proactive action, over time, massively reduces the occurrence of incidents/events in InfoSec.)

Instead we wage a massive yet poorly defined war that cannot be definitively won, because the circumstances work against us. We can win battles, but not the war.

The Information Security threat landscape is no different. Detecting and responding to breaches doesn't eliminate the incentives. Addressing the root causes of the breaches will.

Yes, the above approach might take a generation, a long time. But while we think our approach is a quick one, the fact is the war on terror (the official one) has now lasted nearly 20 years with no end in sight. We could have been done by now, and all been a lot better off. The same situation is present in InfoSec, and the same mind-set must be applied.

And now back to my original point: I cannot fathom a way that terrorists could have inflicted $6,000,000,000,000 of economic damage to the United States itself, no matter how hard they tried (it's more than a hundred 9/11s combined).

When we spend disproportionate amounts of resource dealing with a problem (which we should measure both as total spending *and* effectiveness in reducing the issue over time – which in InfoSec is *a lot* for the former and *none whatsoever* for the latter) we might just be harming our businesses as much if not more than what we're supposed to be fighting!

This is where accountability comes in.

I have horror stories about wasteful InfoSec spending. I don't mean inefficient due to the approach, but downright negligent, verging on criminal.

We have to apply servant leadership and put the organisation's needs before ourselves. It's only logical as we're only there to serve the organisation. If we are draining the organisation's resources without providing real assurance, we are harming the business rather than helping it.

I repeat.

"We are draining the organisation's resources without providing real assurance..." I want everyone to be honest with themselves and reflect hard on this.

Imagine you were a general. Imagine that your organisation's resources (money, people, etc.) are like soldiers.

Sometimes a general has to make decisions that can send these soldiers to their deaths. These are tough decisions, decisions made with extreme reluctance because of an appreciation of those resources, their value, and the simple strategic consideration that they may be needed on other fronts. Aside from the human cost, there's no point wasting a hundred thousand men to win a battle when it risks losing the war due to being unable to fight on other fronts.

Every dollar InfoSec spends is a dollar that cannot be spent on product development, staff, marketing, sales, customer support, advertising, employee benefits, pensions, and more. Competitive margins can be extremely slim, and a relatively small amount can sometimes send an organisation over the tipping point of non-competitiveness.

I hear CISOs wanting an extra million dollars in budget while wasting, either directly or through inefficiencies, that much or more. They must realise that's more than 20 people's salary. 20 people that could have had a significant impact to the business by boosting R&D, sales, marketing, support, etc. Your budget request could indirectly cost 20 people their job, costing the company work output, and potentially initiating an eventual downward spiral.

I have seen instances such as the NHS where reactive security spending is in the hundreds of millions, yet little to no investment in proactive improvements such as process that would have delivered better assurance at $1/10^{th}$ the cost. How many nurses and doctors couldn't be hired because of those wasted InfoSec hundreds of millions? Thousands. What about medications or equipment? How many people had to wait for treatment, or possibly died as a result of irresponsible InfoSec spending?

Both in business and in InfoSec we should be highly attune to the above. We need to leverage every advantage, every cost benefit, every saving, every efficiency gain we can. All the time. Obsessively. We must avoid being a burden at all costs.

Think also of opportunity cost, not just direct cost; If a security action can reduce $50,000 of risk at a cost of $20,000, then that is a good investment... Unless the marketing department or another part of the business can turn that $20,000 investment into a $100,000 gain, then InfoSec is best letting the business spend that money on what's needed to make that gain since it outweighs what we can contribute by reducing risk.*

Be aligned with business strategy and objectives. Understand their needs and opportunities so you can consider them. Be prepared to *reduce* your budget when it's in the business' interest. Yes, *reduce*.

Make helping the organisation reach its primary goal *your* primary goal, rather than just "doing security."

*I personally dislike this kind of risk calculation as there's simply no good way to put a dollar figure on risk, no matter what Risk Management approaches say. But, since being proactive means there's often not that much spend to begin with, we don't have to be nearly as concerned about accurate risk ROI figures to calculate investment. It doesn't really matter though as long as you just do one thing consistently: Help the business win.

Metrics

I don't like metrics. By which I mean those senior management level InfoSec metrics.

They nag me for the same reasons I discussed in the "Secure Like A Hacker" and "Technical Truth: Integrity" chapters.

We're compounding imperfect and highly arbitrary numbers on top of each other *and* an imperfect foundation, then interpreting them as fact. It's the same kind of reasoning that causes things to be missed and breaches to happen. To me, it doesn't seem like a good way to measure security for the same reason.

Metrics work fine if you want to count simple tangible things. But InfoSec is, by nature, anything but. If anything, any number must be constantly questioned.

But for some reason we like to use metrics to put numbers around complex things. Things that can rarely be quantified. Maybe some can be quantified, but when we start meshing different counts together, assigning our own level of *arbitrary importance* and *assumed accuracy* (which is the difference between InfoSec metrics and ones in more tangible areas like engineering) to each, metrics start becoming pretty useless in a hurry. Not to mention the fact that they tend to not take into account important factors such as culture, human engagement, traction, etc. These factors are often, you guessed it, hard to measure.

I hear you. "Oh, but they want *hard* metrics, not some interpretive number or opinion!" But the fact is many if not virtually all combined/cumulative security metrics are open to interpretation and full of assumptions. Heck, they are the cumulative result of multiple layers of completely arbitrary interpretation.

We can skew hard numbers to say anything we want by raising or lowering the importance of any item or cutting off the top and bottom X percent for "normalisation" reasons (where X is whatever number brings the result closer to what you want). If you honestly explain the reality of Information Security and how wildly inaccurate and even completely misleading the metrics can be, your management is going to be hard pressed to keep asking you for them.

One of my favourite case-in-points about metrics: Vendor claims.

On any given day I'll see a vendor ad claiming...

87% of all breaches are caused by <whatever this vendor claims to remedy>

Then, 10 minutes later...

92% of all breaches are caused by <whatever this other vendor claims to remedy>

5 minutes after that...

78% of all breaches are caused by <whatever this third vendor claims to remedy>

And so on, and so forth. For a cumulative % of (after an hour of vendor posts in my feed) something like 1,762% of all breaches, which is of course completely impossible.

(Plus, somehow, they can tell you that the ROI is exactly 346% despite countless immeasurable intangibles and never even having set foot in your business.)

And yet, individually, each claim or number is potentially correct based on how the question is asked, how answers were weighed, and the scope they sampled it against.

That's how lousy InfoSec metrics are, they can say anything you want, in complete detachment from the practical reality, and still technically be accurate.

It's why boards, after having spent half a million GBP/USD/EUR rectifying audit results and passing the follow-up audit with flying colours are surprised when they ask me "So, we know a 10 isn't possible, but where do you think we are on a scale from 1 to 10?" and I answer "A 2, if I'm being generous" while they're expecting something like a 7.

I can get away with not putting together metrics, and being blunt about our position, and having my professional opinion be good enough, because of all the effort I put in engagement, explaining the reality in plain English, and likewise communicating strategy. If you explain and develop trust then the only metric that matters is how much, on a scale of 1 to 10, they trust you to have their back. Because of that approach and building a solid reputation, you become a trusted advisor whose opinion is a lot more accurate and trustworthy than "hard numbers" build on upon layers and layers of inaccuracies and arbitrary interpretations.

When I do assessments on behalf of CEOs, DPOs, Heads of Legal and so on around their information security posture, the bulk of the initial engagement and report is mostly gut, immeasurable things like a lack of process polish, awareness of platforms, that kind of stuff, there are no hard numbers, and it's all they need to know in order to begin actioning things. Not all problems need to be measured to be fixed, and the ability to just get on with fixing it can be the mark of a professional.

So, my advice is to stop with fancy calculated cumulative metrics, or at least keep it to the absolute bare minimum and resist pressure to do more and try to argue for their elimination or reduction. You're wasting time, and abstracting things to the point that you're going to *miss risks*.

I repeat, again... *Engage the business*. This will allow you to know what the state of affairs is, what challenges stand in the way of fixing things, and what the best long-term strategy(ies) to do so might be. Then just tell the board as much. The fact that you've taken the time to explore the business and are thinking long-term will be reassuring to them and give them confidence in you. Confidence that is actually based on something much more real, from a human perspective anyway, than fuzzy math.

When I have to, I give 3 scores from 1 to 10:

Visibility: How much of the estate can I actually see? Or perhaps, how confident am I that I'm seeing everything and how much might I be missing? These are known unknowns and unknown unknowns, there's an element of "gut feel" to it, and that feel is tuned, refined, and made more accurate by getting an idea of what's happening in the business. If every time I lift a rock I find 3 servers that aren't in the asset register, I can guess there are a lot of unknown assets, then, by knowing all parts of the business, how much IT they use, and how likely they each are to display the same behaviour I can start forming rough guesses as to what % of the estate I'm missing.

Capability: Do I have the tooling/resource to find and rectify issues? This is somewhat cyclical with visibility as it can feed into it. (Better discovery capability increases visibility scores, for example.)

Maturity: I can know what systems and issues are there, and I can have all the tools and processes on paper to manage them, but how mature are they? Are they solid processes? Are they performed? Repeatedly? Are they updated? Do they fit together, reinforce and validate each other? That's my Maturity Score.

Sometimes I break these down for different sites or cloud vs on-premise when there are significant enough differences between the metrics (where an average wouldn't represent either site or platform accurately) or very different security strategies apply.

I always give a brief 30 second explanation of each, never just a number, giving practical examples from around the business.

This both helps put context around the number, supporting it, and gives you added credibility by demonstrating, even if at an extremely high level, that you are on top of things. It shows you have a solid understanding of the different parts of the business and are taking them into consideration.

I can give these numbers in the spur of the moment, any time, because I know what's going on and where we are. They're not written down anywhere.

Security in a living breathing organisation isn't hard math, stop wasting time trying to make the math fit the problem and just *know* and address the problem. If you know the problem and you make that clear, you can significantly reduce the pressure [and time lost] to produce metrics.

Compliance to What?

For a while it seemed security was all about compliance, it's what we aimed for, aspired for, and frankly it's what we got budget for.

Business all of a sudden had to get PCI compliant, SOX compliant, ISO 27001, or NIST, or Cyber Essentials, or SOC2, for business, regulatory, and contractual requirements.

It had to be done.

Security people may have been unable to convince their management to spend money on security (assuming we ourselves even really knew what to secure and how) but now there were hard business requirements and the security/compliance dollars flowed.

Except we went to tick boxes and implemented haphazard security to meet the on-paper compliance requirements. We put in "controls."

These didn't truly ensure the ongoing consistency and integrity needed to actually make anything secure. Let's be honest, we all partied a bit buying a bunch of cool kit and the consultants just partied full-stop.

And now we all know that compliance does *not* equal security. Heck, more and more we treat them differently, to the point of having different people and teams handling them.

But what if we've once again railroaded ourselves into a way of thinking, missing out on the bigger picture?

Here's a perhaps stupid-sounding statement: I'd argue that security *can* be achieved through compliance. You could even argue there's no better way to do it.

The question is: Compliance to *what*?

Compliance is a noun. Nothing more. Yet through indoctrination we take it to mean compliance to a handful of 3rd party security "frameworks", or "models", or "systems", or whatever else you want to call it. NIST, ISO, PCI, etc. Those are the things that come to mind.

What if we made compliance not about complying to those things, but complying to what we, ourselves, after engaging our organization, careful thought, review, and agreement have decided is best for *us*? Complying to the rules, processes, and standards that would work for us, that would ensure the integrity of *our* environment and business. Operating with well-defined, fitted, and highly granular instructions, rather than generic tick-boxing from a 3rd party standard created by people who don't have the first idea about our business?

What if we built security compliance that fit our precise business processes, rather than some generic third-party standard that's always going to be more cumbersome to align?

Let me ask you this: When you implement ISO 27001 or any other significant security certification, as generic as it is, do you find you have gaps? Of course you do, it's the first step of the certification process, performing a gap analysis to find where you're missing processes and controls.

Now, why did you have gaps? Whatever stopped you from engaging every part of the business and the IT lifecycle and making sure you had security that fit well before? Why did we not have a look before we were forced to by the compliance exercise?

There's no reason, and it's fundamental to how most big breaches happen, things get missed, despite being certified compliant to NIST, ISO, whatever. You didn't have gaps because you didn't have a 3rd party compliance standard/ISMS in place, you had gaps because you never looked.

When we bring the 3rd party compliance standard in, the one that knows nothing about our specific situation, it's obviously not going to cover everything we have, which means we'll still miss things. We're not going to look at every part of our business while we're focused on looking at the 3rd party compliance standard instead.

It gets better though. Because even if we assumed that compliance brought security (which, if you're using a generic 3rd party standard, it likely doesn't) what happens after you've put in all the money and effort to get certified?

What happens 11 months later when the external auditor is about to come for a visit to do a surveillance audit or recertification?

Everyone scrambles to update dates on documents, catch up on work that wasn't done, deprioritise certain risks as to not raise the question of why they haven't been addressed, clean up some low-hanging fruit, and generally make things look passable.

Tell me I'm wrong.

This is proof that the supposed security function (say "ISMS") of that compliance certification isn't working. That certification therefore isn't worth the paper it's printed on.

Do you think some attacker is going to schedule when they're going to hack you to give you time to spruce things up beforehand?

"Hello? Yes, this is APT47. Listen, we were thinking of hacking you next month, is the 17th a good date? Yeah? Uhm, say 2pm? Ok, great, see you then."

Of course not. The whole thing is idiotic, and I can sum it up as follows:

If your audit preparation consists of anything more than reserving a parking spot for the auditor, you have failed.

You are effectively lying to the auditor and lying to yourself and your organisation.

So how can we make compliance actually work for security?

Well, as we discussed earlier, it's about what we're trying to be compliant to. The answer is: what's best for us.

This is the simple argument behind creating our own framework, a framework that works best for us.

(As I said I will dedicate and entire future book in this series focusing on this, but I will try to give a quick overview on the creation of a bespoke framework later in the final chapters of this book as a starting point.)

Obviously, even if we have the perfect kind of compliance, the kind that allows us to provide much higher levels of assurance than any 3rd party standard and to be far ahead of the curve, the fact is we still have to play by some of the industry's rules for business reasons, no matter how backwards those rules may be. We still have regulatory and/or contractual requirements.

The good news is that once you've mapped your security compliance to *your* business through a bespoke framework, it's very easy to quickly map other 3rd party standards to it, and you'll always be able to justify and prove the existence of any controls.

That means a few things happen:

Firstly, the "extra effort" to develop a custom framework is more than made up by the reduced effort to maintain it. Because of its integration into and alignment with business/IT processes, the framework's security measures naturally get executed as part of business process rather than as an additional layer (which is always the first to get dropped). Consistency can be assured by the nature and integration of the processes themselves.

Secondly, compliance efforts to outside standards become a breeze as these can be rapidly mapped to a comprehensive and effective existing framework closely integrated into the business, with all the needed controls and justifications.

This last bit becomes a significant competitive advantage to the business, especially when moving into new international markets subject to different standards and/or regulations. It can lower barriers to entry while competitors struggle with implementing new compliance standards nearly from scratch.

It also means you reduce your operational reliance on standard-specific experts and their associated costs.

I've been responsible for maintaining and in some cases obtaining ISO 27001, SOX, Cyber Essentials Plus, and PCI compliance in a number of organisations. I must confess that I've never really read any of them in depth, other than a brief pre-audit touch-up.

By building your programme around the business on the back of holistic engagement, you already know you have security built around all of your business processes.

This meant there won't really be any gaps, and anything that doesn't line up with what a particular 3rd party standard wants as a "control" can always be attributed to something else. Not as a *compensating* thing, but because it's actually a *better* fit to the business than what was prescribed, regardless of the standard applied.

Now it's true that the mapping can sometimes be cumbersome, certainly the first time. That said, once the auditors see the level of business alignment and integration, it's usually pretty smooth sailing from there.

I rather put a little effort explaining those mappings and having the actual execution of the security be aligned and straightforward (and therefore basically on autopilot) than vice versa.

Remember though that the mapping is the *only* work we have to do, there is typically no implementation work required at all to reach that 3rd party compliance provided you went far enough in *your* bespoke framework.

That is a significant reduction in compliance spending over time, further complimenting the savings achieved by the proactive/upstream security approach.

Compliance as a Brand

As a perhaps different perspective to the last chapter, I figured I'd include the following LinkedIn article I wrote last year (with some slight edits). Here goes.

Recently, while I was explaining all the issues I found in organisations despite their ISO 27001, PCI or CAS(T) certifications to a friend outside of IT (and therefore free of some of the indoctrination), he made a comment to me about what he called the "Ralph Lauren factor" with relation to compliance. He put things into a new context that I'd never thought of around compliance: It's a *brand* issue.

ISO 27001 is a recognisable *brand*. My friend said he could be wearing an awful sweater, but if it had "Ralph Lauren" written across it, then people will think "It must be good." We all know this is how brands work, but I'd never thought about compliance this way.

He's right, and the same problem is true of frameworks, products, buzzwords, certifications, etc. Many people in this industry that should understand the subject matter don't, and instead rely on a brand.

I had a tailor in Bologna that made me made-to-measure suits for a certain amount. I know for a fact that the materials, cut, quality, and fit was superior to any Gucci suit costing twice as much (they aren't even fully canvassed!), but the layman that doesn't know the intricacies of suits, fabrics, and tailoring will look at the

Gucci suit and assume it's better. The layman has faith in the brand, he doesn't understand the detail. He will end up getting an inferior product, at a much higher cost, for the brand.

One day the Gucci-buying layman will be standing in an elevator in London next to a guy in a perfect no-name suit, and he'll feel smug as people notice the Gucci logo on his buttons and give him a nod. But should those elevator doors ever open and a Saville Row tailor step in, he'll be caught out when the tailor gives Mr bespoke-no-name-suit a nod, instead of him. He'll then see the tailor give him (Mr Gucci) a passing glance only to share a knowing smirk with Mr no-name.

And herein lies the problem. Your Gucci compliance may please auditors and executives, but the people trying to break into your organisations don't care about your branded buttons and logos, that's not that stops them; they care about the details, not the logo. What stops them is good materials, great fit, quality construction, and perfect seams. They don't even look at the brand, it doesn't matter to them (read: your certificates on the wall aren't keeping you secure).

And this is where the "Compliance does not equal security" argument becomes interesting. Because, what is compliance? Is it *only* brand-name compliance?

Is a perfect no-name suit not a suit? My closet says it is, and I prefer getting recognition from the handful that understand, because they're the ones that matter. I want to be secure, not win a popularity contest.

If I'm a tailor, a craftsman, dedicated to the perfect creation that fits every one of my clients, I can't have a one-size-fits-most template. I will have a custom design for every client. And my suit will be perfectly compliant to that design. It just won't have a generic brand associated to it.

So, what if we stopped weighing compliance by its brand and instead focused on its fit and quality, since that's what provides actual protection, that's what eliminates the imperfections and gaps that let attackers in?

What if compliance could equal security, if we made it about compliance to the perfect template? A made to measure template, built just for us? What if we just grew up as an industry and switched to good clothes instead of branded clothes? What if we stopped caring about the brand and acquired enough knowledge to judge a suit like a tailor? By its fabric, cut, stitching, the way it falls, instead of by an almost meaningless label?

Is it not time that our security be compliant, perfectly fitted, to *our* business?

Ah! "But we need ISO 27001 for business reasons" I hear you say. Well here's the beauty of it: Once you have a perfect suit that outperforms everything Gucci has, for half the price, it's quite easy (and cheap) to sow on some Gucci buttons and a name on the tag. The laymen will think you have a great Gucci suit, but you'll know you have something much better... and the tailor will give you the nod. Not even Gucci will complain, because you're making *them* look good.

Engage and learn about your business, your organisation, your people. Build them the perfect suit. Then simply sow on the branded buttons if your business or clients require them.

You're the only one that can know what fits your business best, you just need to get handy with the tape measurer and the needle.

Audits

While we're talking about compliance, let's talk about audits.

Ah, audits.

Let's be honest. They're crap.

The things I've seen companies (and their IT & InfoSec departments) slide past the "Big 4" boggles the mind.

It's not difficult either, most auditors miss stuff you'd be hard pressed not to trip over repeatedly without even trying. It's the kind of stuff the Star Trek Picard/Riker double facepalm meme was created for.

I've lost count of the number of times I walked into an organisation that has held multiple compliance accreditations, certified by one of the Big 4 for years, and within an hour (and sometimes 5 minutes) found major systematic security issues that had been there for years.

As an aside... Ironically, and perhaps as a worrisome indicator as to Information Security culture, this is usually when I'm asked to leave. Companies and their InfoSec departments are happiest when you find nothing, or at most small incremental improvements, as it makes them look good. Finding issues in new areas can also be good when you are commissioned to do so. But when you find issues, big issues, big systematic long-present issues in areas they've long been satisfied with, that's when I find my consulting/assessment engagements quickly terminated by Heads of InfoSec/CISOs and IT. It's why I do assessments exclusively for C-levels, Heads of Legal, law firms, and DPOs; those charged with security are often the least interested in improving security.

Perhaps the Big 4 are a lot smarter than I give them credit for. Perhaps they've figured it out and that's why they're so good at not finding things. Maybe that's actually a conscious strategy for how they stay in business, keep getting asked to come back, and able to bill so much money.

But as "bad" as they may be, we have to be honest about something: We, InfoSec practitioners, lie to the auditors.

The fact that we do audit preparation, trying to close items, update registers, fix issues before they show up, try to divert their attention, and embellish what we present is a sign that we're not doing our jobs when people aren't looking.

Again. We're lying to them, and we're lying to ourselves.

If your security programme requires you to do this, it isn't working.

Conversely, if you still need to develop and mature your security organisation, why are you lying about it? Outside auditors have tremendous traction with management, risk committees, and the board. You can use their findings to further your objective of protecting the business (assuming that *is* your objective), to gain support and visibility.

I find it strange that CISOs fight constantly to be heard about how they need help, support, and resource, then, when someone comes along that has the board's ear and can help them, they try to paint a rosy picture and cover up the issues they need help with.

Use the auditors, feed them the info, stop complaining that the board only listens to them and leverage that fact to steer them towards what you need.

Stop trying to save face. Be honest.

Engage the business so you can actually discover the issues. Then formulate an actual plan, a detailed strategy, and tell the auditor about it and what the hold-up is.

Your audit report will read: "You have serious issues, your CISO has fed us lots of information, they clearly know what they're doing and have a solid strategy to resolve, but they need the following..."

What do you think happens next? Instead of trying to dodge a beating you can stand tall and get support.

Stop hating audits, stop hiding things from your auditors. If you're doing everything you can you shouldn't have to.

Instead, leverage your audits for traction towards your security strategy.

Security Value

Security spend is not security value.

Too many boards (and security organisations) have this understanding, and too many companies advertise "We will spend X million" on security to reassure the public after a breach.

I cringe every time, because I know they'd probably get more value out of that money if they burned it to heat up some water for a cup of tea. Literally. We'll discuss in the next chapter.

And who's to blame for this?

Well the security industry certainly loves it; it's big money. It allows this circular bubble economy of setting up security companies that can collect huge revenue due to the sheer amounts of money being spent, then get hyped-up and sold-off or IPO'd before they collapse like a bad soufflé... Only to soon be replaced by the next big thing. The Beyond-next-next-next-Gen Blinkybox 9000 or whatever.

The more stable "blue chip" players are less profiteering but obviously gain from it to.

But while vendor-shaming can be fun, I'm also going to argue it's us, the security practitioners, especially the ones in senior and "leadership" roles.

We're not informing management of how most security spending is a money pit, and often it's because the CISO benefits even more than the vendors.

I've seen many an Ivory Tower being built with security money. I've seen my share of terrible, often toxic, "leaders" building up large teams to give themselves importance and even bigger budgets, usually completely disconnected from the organisation's needs, having little care for the people they manage or the business as a whole.

Yet they are often incredibly "successful" in terms of pay and status, merely by weaving a web of bullshit to senior management and silencing anyone (including their own people) daring to step out of their silo to point out something might not be right.

Make no mistake about it, there are a lot of awful CISOs out there, doing nothing more than profiting personally while damaging the very organisations that rely on them. The MSP market in particular seems rife with them.

Somewhat less sinister is not informing senior management of how much more cost-effectively we could be doing things. Most of the time it's simply because we don't know any better.

It's up to us to take our head out of the industry sandbox, look around, and start developing some real value.

A lot of that is achievable through leadership and a proactive approach.

We work for the business, not just security. It's not us vs them. We owe it to the business, everyone that works there, and to our professional ethos to offer effective and *cost*-effective security. To use as little as we can, do as much as we can, and give back everything we don't need.

It's our job to provide value.

Burn Your Money

Let me share an article I wrote a couple years back...

I saw the resume of a CISO last week.

The first thing listed under his accomplishments was how he had gotten his last employer to significantly increase InfoSec spending.

I can already hear everyone say, "Well done!"

Are we sure though?

On my resume, I talk about *reducing* spending.

Seriously, who thinks spending *more* money is a good thing?

I often talk about a case where a company had spent more than £1,000,000 on a SIEM service that was monitoring *zero* systems. Would they have been more secure if they had wasted more money?

Just this week I overhead a new-in-role CISO mention they had requested hundreds of thousands of pounds of funding for things within a couple of weeks of starting. I was surprised they even knew what they needed so early in, and that the initial issues weren't buy-in, process, or culture related. They finally agreed but said their company's budget cycle was closing and so they just "had to put in something" and so they did. No way was that optimised spending.

Make no mistake about it. I have never walked into a large established company and thought their information security was underfunded... no matter how poor their security posture was. To the contrary, they typically had significant (if not mind-boggling) amounts of waste.

Reducing that waste, through better visibility and synergy, probably improves security more than spending another half a million on tools and technologies.

A lot of the really insecure companies out there, the ones often suffering massive breaches, are not the ones spending too little money on InfoSec. They're often the ones spending lots. Too much spending, not enough thinking. Having too much money does that. Being forced to be frugal makes people not just get creative, but also makes them address more fundamental issues. Issues that often have the highest impact, and don't have significant costs to resolve.

Yes, at some point, with the right criteria, you can estimate how effective an organisation's Information Security is by how *cheap* it is. Let that sink in for a minute.

Most of the organisations I've worked with could have done a significantly better job securing things while spending half of their current budgets. I mean that wholeheartedly.

High InfoSec spending is a likely indicator of waste. If you had good visibility and operational efficiency (core requirements for any InfoSec foundation) you wouldn't have that kind of waste.

As I write this chapter, a friend of mine, Eric Parent, just published an article about vetting your vendors. It's unrelated, however it did have this paragraph in it about the Marriott hack:

"This is a large multinational corporation with resources. The breach appears to have gone on for years. In the next few weeks we will see the same list of errors that have been made time and time again by all these corporations that get hit hard. I will take any bets on the presence of some basic fundamental issues being a large contributing factor. They had some great security in place, but a lot of it was tuned down because they don't understand the technology they bought. They have a great big security team, so they feel so great about their security posture yet senior management didn't listen to them. Some of their partners may even have mentioned some significant issues, but the messenger was shot and the message died a slow death. You name it, they['ll] fit the profile."

He is, of course, in all probability, 100% correct. I've seen the same thing in large organisations time and time again.

He cites several reasons why this breach happened despite their investment and Information Security resources. Now read it again and think of the solutions for all the problems/causes he mentions. They all have something in common: They don't cost a dime.

And yet in the coming weeks I expect every other vendor in the security space to cite this hack to try and sell us more stuff. And Marriott will probably try to placate us by saying they will spend another X million dollars to make sure they're secure. Just like the NHS and Equifax did, spending hundreds of millions on impressive security tech.

But not one will mention all the basic IT management and visibility issues that, if addressed, would have prevented this and countless other large breaches, without having to issue a single purchase order. And none of them will focus on fixing those issues that were responsible all along.

We keep the commercial cycle going but never truly solve the problem.

One of the best pieces of advice I can give to many organisations is this:

Zero out your InfoSec budget for 6 months.

The InfoSec organisation will freak out, but after a week they'll wonder what they should be doing.

With no more new toys to buy they'll be forced to start looking at what they already have, maximise the use of existing tools, improve the way they're deployed, review processes, even talk to business stakeholders and discover all kinds of assets and business processes they weren't even aware of and were completely failing to protect. All with a net contribution to assurance far higher than the budget you just zeroed out was contributing.

So yes, burn your money. It might just be your best security investment.

Shifting the Value Equation

A little thought exercise about how fundamentally proactive security changes tooling priorities. (Sorry vendors!)

Something interesting happens when we address issues proactively. The order in which we prioritise investments and actions changes.

Let's say an average analyst costs me £50k. In order to handle the number of incidents my SOC sees I need 20 analysts.

My SOC staffing cost is 20 x £50k = £1,000,000.

Now if a tool is available for £200,000 that reduces my workload by 50%, that means I can shed (or reassign) half my headcount.

So now my costs are 10 x £50,000, + £200,000 for the tool. For a total of £700,000. A saving of £300,000.

That makes solid financial sense. This kind of tooling should be a priority as it generates huge savings.

Except for this: What if, by taking a proactive approach (tailoring my security to business processes and having airtight asset management, provisioning, project involvement, patching, host & network configuration management, etc.), combined with fully leveraging human potential and optimizing roles, I can eliminate 90% of the issues upstream?

That means I can now run the SOC with 2 people. (And by the way, this is not an impossible reduction if you go full-in on the approaches discussed in this book)

2x £50,000 = £100,000.

Does it still make sense to spend £200,000 to halve a workload that costs me only half that amount?

No, of course it doesn't.

Detection and response is necessary. But we need to leverage it to spot issues, then chase down their root causes and address them. This is how we do proactive continuous improvement.

Instead we typically merely respond to symptoms, and this is the reason the workload never stops growing.

Aside: I am currently managing Information Security for an organisation of 30,000 users just fine with a team of 2. One spots incidents, the other traces down the root causes and engages the stakeholders so that we can correct the process, while I create the structure and traction to make that possible. And we do it on a budget that is less than a tenth of the market average. – Do not underestimate the power of this proactive approach.

I've lost track of the number of times security sales people pitch me about all the problems people in my role face and how they have a myriad of solutions to help me. Line by line I reply "Sorry, we just don't have that problem, because we addressed X upstream."

You should see their confused expressions, as they try to understand what I just told them, some of them, occasionally, even realise the logic of it and I enjoy watching the look of epiphany on their faces.

Sometimes I watch those faces as they start to formulate a rebuttal, stop mid-sentence realising how the proactive approach mitigated whatever other reason they had for me to buy their product as well, then try to find their place in this new reality.

It's a game changer, and one reason it's so important to come into this approach with a completely open mind, because every part of our approach fundamentally impacts every other.

A lot of the naysayers point to other areas to try and argue that it's impossible, not realising those areas would also be changed by the approach.

Procurement

We've talked about delivering value and needing less through leadership and a proactive approach. But saving a bundle of money on the things we *do* need isn't a bad idea either!

Let's talk procurement.

Procurement processes are typically designed to promote more competitive prices and ensure fairness among bids.

They are probably one of the single biggest sources of waste as well as drivers of corruption and price inflation.

It starts when we create bureaucratic processes stating, for example, that anything needed should be specified then sent to 3 different vendors or providers for quotes, and that we then take the lowest of those quotes/bids for the service provided.

So, we need something for project X and therefore send out 3 requests for quotes to 3 different vendors.

One bids £250,000, one £220,000 and one £280,000.

We go for the one that's £220,000 and as such saved at least £30,000 over the nearest bid. Well done procurement process person!

Except you could have negotiated any one of these vendors down to £50k or less, with better SLA's, better support, fewer avenues for "nickel and diming", and just generally lower costs, immediate and ongoing, in half the time it took you to run these vendors through your process. And now that you've formally locked in a vendor, you've lost all your bargaining power.

Tack on the fact that technical, operational, legal, support, and all kinds of other issues are typically woefully defined in procurement processes and tenders, and organisations often end up stuck in situations where they massively overpay for services for years, and often end up paying even more for "extras" that should have been included all along.

With many bigger vendors, 80+% discounts, plus extras, are perfectly routine when it comes to software solutions provide you use the right negotiating approach. And I'm not talking end of quarter or end of year stuff either. By getting vendors emotionally invested in the sale you can usually get them to cave significantly on pricing.

The aforementioned procurement and tender processes also encourage the creation of cartels and price-fixing, especially in the public sector. (I've had more than one vendor fess up to this privately after a few pints!)

Fortunately for us, the security market is so oversaturated with vendors that there are virtually always alternatives. When they haven't been ruled out by cumbersome overthought procurement "vetting" and "vendor management" processes designed to keep things fair, that is. Oh, the irony.

With public institutions (here in the UK at least) in particular we have the interesting practice of "frameworks" where several institutions will band together to get a better deal. In theory.

The same problems apply once again, but things get even worse. Firstly, the bureaucracy is even higher, but there is also a loss of flexibility, and all buying parties must compromise in such a way that often not a single one of them gets a solution or terms that are actually ideal for them.

Nope. When I encounter this kind of cumbersome procurement process, I always sidestep it. Sometimes procurement gets angry with me, but time after time they can't come close to the prices I managed to negotiate (next chapter) and it becomes hard for them to argue.

If they insist, just make the CFO your friend. It probably won't be hard when you're saving them hundreds of thousands, millions in some cases.

Human relationships trump everything.

Vendor Negotiations

To me the relationship with a vendor is important. I want them to care, I want them to have a clear philosophy behind their product, their services, and how they treat their relationship with me, their customer.

There are vendors out there with solutions that may be best of breed, but they won't try to help out, quote you an arm and a leg, try and bill you for every little thing, and good luck getting anything done in terms of support unless you've paid outlandish fees for premium support and even then it can be a roll of the dice.

Then there are vendors that care about their clients, that believe in their products, that will make things work for you and your budget, and that enjoy a good *personal* relationship with you. Vendors that have reasonable prices *and* will come right out of the gate with heavy discounts on top of that before you've even started whittling things down because they want to help.

Relationships are important. As are negotiations. But be aware that negotiating is not just about asking for a lower price, it's a psychological process and you have to play on their emotional investment in the sale just as much as they're trying to play on yours. You have options, they have competitors, leverage it, leverage brand exposure, leverage positive PR, leverage your own personal reputation if you have one (think LinkedIn), leverage market share, leverage everything you can to get a better deal out of them.

Too many organisations underestimate their value to vendors. It's not just the revenue from the immediate sale. It's adding clients to their portfolio, it's locking you in and potentially upselling you later, it's gaining market share, it's getting more feedback that can go into marketing and product improvements, it's exposure.

They *want* to sell you their product or service, even if you're just a little fish, possibly far more than you want or even need their product.

There's a reason why vendors go out of their way to get in touch with us, to pitch us, to take us to conferences, to buy us dinner, and more.

Leverage it.

Payroll

The other big areas of security spending is of course, on salaries (and contractors/professional services).

We've discussed how we can do a lot more with fewer people by taking a strategic proactive approach. Obviously, this is going to translate to a reduction in payroll. But what about the people we do need?

Firstly let me say that I believe it's generally far better for the overall capability of the organisation to hire 3 people at 30k than one at 100k.

The argument has always been that the one earning 100k has the experience and is therefore worth the money. But in my experience, for many (but not all) roles, this doesn't necessarily apply.

The interesting thing is you don't even need to hire 3 to replace the one "senior" role/candidate. In many cases *one* 30k resource can outperform one earning three times as much if deployed effectively. I've replaced a 150k per year contract resource with a graduate on 1/5th the pay, and the graduate, as a whole, is outperforming the contractor.

If your role is a strategic one and you can act as a force multiplier and cost reducer, then you have the possibility of delivering large-scale change. That change can make the organisation as a whole far more cost-effective to the order of tens of times your salary premium or more. In such a case a salary premium may be worthwhile.

But, at least currently, most roles are operational, and siloed. There's little strategic value to them. Years of experience in many roles doesn't bring significantly more value. Not enough to justify the salary premium.

This doesn't mean we should just suddenly pay people less, that would be rather disruptive! Instead we need to push and enable them to perform more proactive roles that can deliver higher value.

One of the big ironies here is that, going back to the car factory analogy, – and forgive me as I'll probably repeat this a few times in the book – if I hire the average 10-year CISSP he/she will likely make a beeline for the parking lot and start swapping body panels and suspension assemblies. Meanwhile, a graduate that costs a quarter as much would immediately start asking questions as to why the hell we're dropping cars from the 3rd floor.

I think we're at an interesting moment in the sector in terms of resourcing. While we are pushing for millions more bodies to enter the workforce, the reality is that, if we did things efficiently and proactively, we'd already have a massively oversaturated security workforce.

Then there's the fact that, despite everyone screaming for more bodies, many seem extremely reluctant to hire people relatively new to the field. The ones that do rarely put in the effort to mentor them in order to get much out of them, stifling their growth instead.

The number of security professionals that are completely averse to taking on junior staff is disconcerting and frankly upsetting. This is made even more absurd by the fact that many of these "junior" resources could be operating mid-level roles within months.

The result of this is that we have an unprecedented amount of tremendous talent, whether they be young people just entering the workforce or older people transitioning from other fields, desperately looking for work, incredibly eager, and happy to take entry level salaries. It's a tremendous opportunity for those of us willing to take them on.

We just have to be willing to let them do the work. It's really that simple barring having to put in a little time towards guiding and mentoring, which is actually hugely rewarding and is often the best part of being a boss.

Teach them resiliency, autonomy, give them confidence but let them know where the limits are, let them know you are available whenever they need you, and have their back if something goes wrong or someone gives them a hard time. Do this and you will have "junior" employees with little to no experience outperform the average veteran practitioner within a couple of months, for a third of the salary.

What about retention? Glad you asked.

Retention

When I put "cyber retention" into google, the first suggestions that come up before I even hit enter are:

Cyber retention pay
Cyber retention bonus

This and several other variations. All are about *money*.

My current role at the University of Salford has just about the most ridiculous cyber security budget you could imagine.

We have virtually no tooling budget and, for staffing, I was given enough budget to hire *one* mid-level security analyst. I split that money in half and hired two high-performing individuals. High-performing individuals the market says are of low to no value and therefore available at a bargain (financially) when you compare it to their potential output.

I have a team of two. To manage 30,000 users, most of whom pay to be there and are therefore treated as customers, and many others that demand whatever they want whenever they want. Users that are very transient, about 1/3rd annual turnover, and dozens of completely different research and industry collaboration departments with vastly different requirements that change on a daily basis.

Most people would imagine this to require significant manpower and be highly stressful to stay on top of issues, meaning retention money is an important factor.

Yet I don't feel this team of two and myself are overly stressed. (We've already discussed why so many security departments are overstaffed and yet massively stressed.)

Their pay packages for what they do are significantly below industry averages. (Although the pension is pretty good.)

And it's not just them. When I look at Glassdoor, I'm so far off the bottom end of the scale that it's not even funny.

So why am I able to do this? And why don't they (or I) leave? Because they are the kind of individuals the current marketplace snubs despite having abilities that, in my opinion, are more valuable than those of the average Information Security person earning far more.

Both the members of my team could probably earn near double the money in 3 years' time. Heck, possibly sooner. The Irony is that no one in the industry would believe what they're capable of after "only 3 years' experience" in the industry (when the reality is they had those skills after 3 months).

Am I worried about them leaving then? No. I'll eventually get them an increase. It'll still be well below market rate, and they'll likely be happy to stay because there's even more growth in it for them.

Eventually they *will* leave the nest so to speak and go out to make some of that big security money. When they're ready for that move I will help them on their way to find a new job that suits and appreciates them. Yes, I will put effort in to help them leave. I'll give them advice, help them write their CV, write recommendations, advertise them to my LinkedIn network, etc. Even today I try to point things out that we do differently to most places so that they're better prepared for their *next* job, and try to get them noticed on LinkedIn so they have a presence when they need one.

I'll be sorry to see them go, but there is a massive queue of new talent ready to take their place, and it'll be fun and rewarding to bring them up to speed, to grow a whole new team (hopefully with some overlap this time).

By the way, I don't buy the argument of the time and cost to train people. My team trained themselves on all tooling, went out and learned the organisation with minimal support. Just find the right people, the ones that want to learn, rather than the ones that tick all the role boxes.

My philosophy is to give them the most senior work you can, just give it to them one step at a time, touch point at every step of the way, and soon enough they'll have achieved what should be a "senior" task far beyond what people would think they'd be up to.

Throw them in the deep end of the pool, just always be there if they need a hand.

Bottom line? Stop worrying about making people stay with money and become a half decent leader to them so they don't want to run away in the first place.

Most people rather have a better boss than a better salary.

Here's something I pulled out of an article if you don't believe me:

Employee engagement firm TINYpulse found that money ranked a lowly seventh place on the list of factors that motivate employees to go the extra mile, with only 7% of the 200,000 workers surveyed listing it as a motivating factor.

That puts it behind camaraderie and peer motivation (20%), intrinsic desire to do a good job (17%), feeling encouraged and recognized (13%), having a real impact (10%), growing professionally (8%) and meeting client and customer needs (8%).

Clearly, we see that many factors are at play when it comes to motivating your team, but when managers and leaders and those in HR responsible for overall company motivation get it right, the rewards can be, well, incredibly rewarding.

Just how much so? According to Dr. Stephen Covey, in his book The 7 Habits of Highly Effective People, the difference between "poorly motivated and highly motivated employees is about 500% in productivity. "

That last bit is staggering, but if I think back I can say I've certainly seen that. A 500% difference in productivity between low output and high output employees, and money is only 7% of that difference! The interesting thing is that the things that make people produce 5 times the output are the same things that will make them want to stay. And it's not money.

Heck, money can even *decrease* output.

Studies have shown that people paid more as an incentive to do a task faster actually performed more slowly!

This is due to what is known as the "over-justification effect." It occurs when external incentives such as money or prizes actually decrease a person's motivation to perform a task, because they begin to pay more attention to the incentive itself, and less to the enjoyment and satisfaction they receive from performing the activity.

This doesn't mean you should use this as an excuse to weasel out of paying people properly, but I rather everyone put in effort catering to motivators 1 through 6 rather than just throw money at the problem. This means you will attract the best talent and the kind of people that are in it to truly contribute, and you can get them on average or lower salaries because they understand the non-financial benefits they're getting, whether that be support, a positive environment, satisfaction, growth, etc.

Stop making things about money.

Many of us, heck I believe statistics show it's most of us, hate where we work.

If we're lucky enough to work somewhere we enjoy, we're not going to give that up and be less happy, possibly miserable, for an extra 10-20% pay. And more and more people are willing to take a pay cut to stop feeling miserable and feel more fulfilled instead.

This is what you should be catering to.

And, while we're here, for crying out loud, it's not about swanky offices, bean bag seating, free afternoon beer, or any of that eye candy. It's about helping people feel valued. It's about enabling them to contribute, make a difference, and be able to see it themselves. It's about helping them grow even if it means they might someday leave, because if you don't they won't contribute nearly as much and quite frankly they're going to leave much sooner anyway due to being unhappy.

It's about having a real human connection. No amount of well funding training and retention programmes are going to make as much of a difference as a positive personal relationship with your people.

Conclusion: You can save on payroll and get multiple times the output by simply being a good leader, creating the right culture, and caring. It feels great too.

Human Potential

I'm not concerned about that "cyber security skills gap", I'm worried about our expectations around potential and the gap caused by how we limit and structure skills.

20-some years ago, when I was a teenage hacker, I would go through a couple of 400-page technical books every week, endlessly search online to learn things, download new operating systems onto old PCs and tear them apart, read through countless Linux and BSD man pages, etc.

I would spend my day on Internet Relay Chat talking with other hackers. It was all very competitive and elitist. I remember lots of kids from all over the place. Turkey, Norway, the UK, Holland, etc. Their English was all perfect. It was such an elitist culture that no spelling or grammar mistake would be tolerated. If you misspelled something they'd rub it in your face and mock you. You had to show you were smart.

Relatively speaking, my rate of knowledge acquisition was staggering during this period. By comparison, I feel like a broken old goat nowadays. I don't see how it could ever have caught up to the level of some of those guys though, they were awe inspiring (although, I now realise, maybe more focalised).

When I was 18, I started picking up a lot of IT/InfoSec certifications. I remember getting one in particular (a

CompTIA post I saw on LinkedIn gave this certification their highest rating: "Expert" level) and telling my online friends about it. Their response when I told them I'd passed the certification exam?

One said: "Congratulations, you can read."

The others laughed.

Compared to what most of these teenage kids figured out by themselves, the highest level of InfoSec certification in the industry is an absolute joke.

Things get really worrisome when you look at how we use and interpret these certifications. I talked about this in the Certifications chapter of this book.

I see a lot of people identifying themselves as experts or qualified because of their certifications. Hackers, including malicious hackers, would laugh them out of the room.

To those hackers, these people not only look ridiculous because they think they've got everything covered when they don't have a clue in the grand scheme of things, like a 2-year-old that thinks it can outrun Usain Bolt at the Olympics because it can hobble from one side of the living room to the other, but also because they've just signalled a level of indoctrination by linking their abilities to a certification. This Indicates an inability to work things out for themselves, to see the big picture, or anything else not spoon-fed to them.

How can they possibly compete?

In the Certifications chapter I explained how they were, at best, a starting point. One to be taken with a dash of salt at that. We really need to shift our perception of scale. These "expert" certifications aren't. They are very, very basic.

There simply aren't *any* certifications that we should consider "Advanced" or "Expert." You become an expert through thinking and experience, by constantly pushing, and in the case of this particular field it's also a moving target, because some of our adversaries are pushing very hard indeed. The more advanced technical things are years out of date by the time they're in a curriculum while the human, strategic, political, problem solving, and soft skills often can't be confirmed with a test.

Interestingly, there are currently no certifications around security leadership. My 3-day course seems to be one of the first attempts into this area, which frankly amazes me.

To get back to another analogy from that article about the level of today's InfoSec certifications, it would be like thinking you know everything about driving because you just got your driver's license, then stepping into a formula one race. You wouldn't even be able to get the tyres warm enough for the car to work.

But I digress. it's not just about certifications, it's the general way job roles nowadays have tiny scopes that worries me.

I feel strongly about this because it's a fundamental part of the problem of why businesses today are vulnerable no matter how much they invest in status quo security. Skills must be broad and overlap if they are to not have security gaps.

Let's go to where I started from to illustrate my thought process. Here is a day in the life of teenage hacker Greg, 20-some years ago.

Fade in to Greg's bedroom on a Saturday morning.

-Wake up (at noon).

-Eat a bowl of Cocoa Puffs.

-Build a PC from some old hardware laying around. (66Mhz 486 DX/2 FTW!)

-Download the latest version of OpenBSD on the other computer. "Secure by default!" (Yeah, not so much...)

-Burn an ISO image and boot the new PC with the CD and install the OS.

-Configure the OS, set accounts and permissions.

-Install any new patches validating their integrity.

-Harden the base configuration.

-Set up services (apache, ssh, ftp, X-windows, etc.).

-Tweak some of the C libraries, fixing certain functions that I didn't think had sufficient input checking.

-Get the damn modem working (#@$! you pppd!) and dial up to the internet without a firewall.

-Download and compile snort.

-Download BitchX (IRC client) source code, edit the code to work with my custom libraries, and compile it. Btw, I can't believe it's still around and maintained!

-Hop on Internet Relay Chat, join several hacking channels and antagonise dozens of elite hackers into trying to hack you.

-Pour another bowl of Cocoa Puffs and watch snort blow up as 20 people suddenly start scanning and trying to break into your system.

-Laugh when they connect to port 80 because "Set up services" above included configuring apache to present an image of MC Hammer with the text "j00 c4n7 h4x 7h1$!!" (Emphasis on *teenage* hacker. Sorry.)

What happened next? Nothing.

Like pebbles thrown at a that 70-ton steel armour plated tank. One by one they gave up. You'd earned their respect on defensive skills alone, because these guys could get into pretty much anything that was running a few services.

This is what I call real security from a technical perspective. None of that academic risk management mumbo jumbo. (Something we should do to cover a handful of remaining issues after having done real security, not grow into some monstrosity trying to stay on top of thousands of issues because we didn't do real security.)

One of the core reason I was able to reach this level of security, as close to 100% as you can get, was my broad knowledge base: Understanding all the parts, I was aware of what a change being made in one of these steps meant for the other steps. The steps were mostly iterative, but sometimes changes in one would require returning to a previous step and changing something or optimising something differently.

I knew all the things I had to do, and being the one doing everything, having knowledge of networking, the OS, and each of the individual services, I knew what I had to take into consideration, no matter what. I saw and understood the full spectrum of technical considerations and all their interactions.

Granted, that was just one system. Organisations now have thousands of systems and so we scaled up the work by breaking down each of those steps and assigning them to different job roles and different people, with narrow and easily commoditised skillsets. Today you have 10 people doing the activities I did on my own back then. Yes, it's relatively easy, and yes, it's scalable.

But that's where the problem starts, because security has to be approached holistically, and no matter how hard the industry and frameworks try to break things down into neat little pieces, the reality is that every one of those areas has interactions, effects, and dependencies on other areas.

The segmentation into different areas and disciplines causes us to lose sight of those areas of interaction. We now have a generation of security professionals with skillsets and job roles that focus on specific areas without going much broader. The seams between those areas fail over time as changes in one area are not always considered by other areas, and adjustments to area A that should be made as a consequence of a change in area B often aren't made.

As a result, cracks form between the areas, between the silos. And obviously these unknown areas are never scoped in terms of monitoring or controls.

This is why I consistently find tons of issues within days, sometimes minutes, when I walk into "mature" and ISO 27001 compliant organisations and start digging with a holistic approach. Hundreds, even thousands, of issues missed by the countless controls in place.

So yes, there are many security tools and disciplines now. Too many nowadays for one person to master. But consider that the basics haven't changed, and that many (most?) of these new tools provide reactive security to catch failures further upstream. Their need can be significantly reduced by building systems, applications, and processes with holistic vision.

Therefore I advocate that, while it may not be reasonable to expect someone to have expert level knowledge in dozens of areas, one must still have a solid understanding of all elements that their area of responsibility comes into contact with, as to fully understand the interactions between them, understanding what may influence what, and making sure invisible gaps in assurance don't form between functional areas. No amount of resource can overcome this problem if those resources are segmented without overlap.

We, as human beings, have the ability to do incredible things, we have the potential to see and understand far more than we currently do.

Let's up our game.

The Skills Shortage

Ah the supposed cybersecurity skills gap. Let me share an article I wrote about this topic back in 2018.

Those that know me will tell you that I passionately want to help people and organisations. I'm also rather unpopular in some circles because I point out how the security sphere sometimes makes dealing with the actual problems almost impossible.

The supposed skill gap, by which I could cynically mean the push by Information Security staffing, training, certification, and other interests to increase budgets and pump in more bodies, is yet another thing further entrenching an approach that is not only not working (as headlines remind us on a daily basis), but actually moving us, attention, and resources away from what works. It's not really their fault since most don't realise, but they and the rest of us are contributing to it.

There is no lack of cybersecurity people. Here are 6 reasons why:

1. Human potential – Most people aren't even reaching 10% of their potential. Whether it's simply a greater understanding of one area, gaining capabilities in multiple areas, or... the holy grail: Reaching a level where they can look at the origins of problems holistically and therefore become transformational forces actually

eliminating root causes (massively reducing the operational InfoSec workload.)

InfoSec management needs to stop wasting time looking for more bodies to enlarge their fiefdom and empower their people's growth instead. Teach them tech, teach them critical thinking, and teach them leadership. If you can't, you shouldn't be leading people. And remember what was said in the Retention chapter: the difference in output between employees can vary by 500% depending on motivation.

2. Roles built around people to leverage maximum value – People don't use the majority of their skills in pigeonholed roles. Spend the time to discover their talents and task them accordingly. The amount of talent and promising potential that is wasted in existing resources is absurd. It is not just a waste of resource, but it's also demoralising to those resources. Quality levels increase when people are given a broader area of work what makes them feel more fulfilled.

3. Organisations structured to make the most of their people – Related to the point above, your people's role and abilities being expanded will be futile if their contributions are wiped out by silos or lost in hierarchy. Streamline and simplify your organisation to create visibility and to allow contributions along horizontals. Also, flatten hierarchy to as few levels as possible (broadening your people's skills – to also include soft skills – will make this easier) and create a culture without hard separations. If an analyst wants to pick up the phone and have a chat with the CISO, there's no reason he/she

shouldn't be able to. This gives vertical transparency and visibility that can massively boost awareness, assurance, nimbleness, and quality levels.

4. Root causes – This is my bread and butter and a theme I have written and talked about many times. It is far too wide a topic to go into in depth here but to sum it up: Most people work on symptoms, not problems. The entire InfoSec Industry is set up to deal with symptoms to drive an endless cycle.

I estimate that significantly more than half of the ongoing operational and project work InfoSec departments deal with can be eliminated entirely by sorting out their root causes. Engage the business and sort these out. You will stop an endless rat race where the InfoSec organisation is too stretched to effectively cover all controls. A reduction in workload means you will have more resources to better address remaining risks, maybe even enough capacity to eliminate their root causes as well.

There are no excuses. Engage, care, learn the common language of executives, hone your presentation skills, communication skills, be altruistic, create goodwill that will give you traction. whatever it takes. Get to the root of issues and work with stakeholders to sort them out. There is a blame culture in Information Security pitting InfoSec against users and management when we are meant to be their protectors. The reality is that this often masks a lack of initiative from InfoSec. Is it always fair? No. But like a good parent, we cannot expect them to come to us, we cannot expect them to meet us half way. We must make the effort to go all the way to them.

Remember the words of Albert Einstein "If you can't explain it simply, you don't understand it well enough.", and the fact that we would be hypocrites if we did not try to understand others' perspective.

5. Tooling – How many organisations have I seen complaining about lack of resources when their people had terrible equipment, laptops so slow they took minutes to switch applications, where they refused to spend $200 on a second screen that would boost someone's productivity by 30-50%? Analysts that spend 60% of their time doing manual reporting in Excel because the company didn't want to spend $1,500 on a software license that automated it (yet were fine spending 7 figures on some misconfigured security tools elsewhere)?

Not providing professionals with decent tools such as a decent laptop or extra monitor, or forcing them to do tedious manual work that can be automated is a waste of their talent, your investment in their salaries, and frankly just hurts morale. In some cases, spending a little on basic tools can be a lot more beneficial than spending a fortune on fancy enterprise systems and the latest big security solution.

6. Mentoring. If you develop the skills, (Don't overlook soft skills!) in your own people, you won't have to go shop for those skills elsewhere. You should be spending more time thinking about developing skills in the people

you have than trying to hire the ones you don't. Stop managing and start leading, you'll be amazed at how easily and quickly they grow, mostly all by themselves if you just let them!

While we're at it, it blows my mind just how averse people are at hiring new talent and developing them.

Create a trusted environment, give them the work, be there when they have questions, and watch them learn in days or weeks what some say requires years of experience. Just take care of your team and trust them to do the work.

That's it, 6 points that can cut your staffing needs in half if not more, and that's barely touching all the efficiency gains you can have by switching to a proactive approach.

Now look in the mirror and ask yourself if you really need more bodies and all the overhead, cost, communication difficulties, and visibility loss that it would entail, or could you maybe deliver a lot more with what you already have?

I bet you can.

Mental Health

I'm no expert on this topic, but I'd like to dedicate a quick chapter to mental health, which is increasingly becoming an issue in the Information Security field.

Stress, burnout, and depression play a prominent role, but why?

Here's what I think are some of the reasons:

Firstly, a lack of good leadership. Specifically, a lack of focus on people, of care, and support.

Not as in these [ironically impersonal] in-house structured support services that are popping up all over the place to make up for the lack or real human care and involvement, but simply as one human being to another.

I've lost track of how many awful bosses I've had. You, as an employee, filled a function and that was it. No personal contact, no concern about the individual (employee). Not even any real interest about their ambitions or interests which could be leveraged to plan their professional progression and a strategy to leverage those skills. Nothing to boost their motivation, satisfaction, usefulness, or to increase the quality of their work.

What do people in these situations do? They get tired and eventually find a new job. Even if the scenario repeats itself they at least get a fresh start, usually a pay or title bump, and the hope things will be better. But I've found that ultimately things stay the same. We may progress on paper, make a little more money, but really most people are just not happy to have to go to work in the morning.

This is nothing new, although it may (or may not) be exacerbated in IT and especially InfoSec because we tend to be even worse with people than most. Which means we make even worse managers.

That said, I believe there is something particular about the way we are doing Information Security that makes matters worse still.

For starters, the fact that we are trying to fit people into pigeon-holed roles, where diversity (as much as we harp on about it) and individual talents are lost (stripped?) and left unexplored and people's sense of self unfulfilled.

But then there's that reactive approach, that approach whereby people spend all their time behind a computer screen handling incident after incident, with no control over their cause, and no end in sight. In fact, the volume will only ever increase.

It's hopeless, and I've heard talks about how many events per day an analyst should handle before considering themselves as having contributed enough. We have to tell ourselves when we've done enough to feel good about! Because we never see actually fixing anything.

We are far more likely to feel satisfied if we actually fix a real [long-term] problem. That means the proactive approach is not just more effective, it's more rewarding.

Furthermore, that proactive approach requires more creative thinking, and more human interaction. Things we crave and need by nature, and we feel good when we do. It's simple biology and psychology.

One more reason to get out of the reactive cycle we're stuck in far downstream of the problem and start proactively fixing problems.

Heck, it's almost like mother nature wants us to.

Hiring: A Case Study

Hiring. Or rather, how I hire, or have hired.

This one is likely to be a little controversial. I wouldn't expect anyone to use these exact methods and quite frankly I haven't really thought this through much so I'm sure there's even better ways of doing this... and yet, despite all this, these random approaches already work so much better than the status quo.

I'm sharing this purely as food for thought. Keep in mind this is the smallest and yet most productive (per head) team I've put together so far.

My first hire at UoS was an operational security person that could handle "Business as Usual" incidents. He is a one-man SOC, coordinates with the service desk, handles change requests relevant to his activities, coordinates with IT on maximising the capability of our IT and InfoSec tools, does the odd bit of forensics, and a few other things.

In short, the bulk of his job is to catch any security events, fight the fires that need fighting, provide feedback on what he's seeing so that the rest of the team can make long-term improvements that keep those security events/incidents from happening in the first place.

When I started this role was handled by a contractor with a £750 gross day rate, and there was no real focus on long-term improvement.

I did not create a job spec as required by HR to start the long and painful standard interviewing/hiring process.

I just posted something on LinkedIn saying I wanted a fresh minded graduate or similar with only the vaguest detail for the role.

I was then contacted and given a young man's CV by a recruiter I didn't know (shout out to Darryl Jones here). He offered it with no strings, free, simply because he knew the person, wanted to help them out, and quite frankly would have struggled to find them anything.

Why?

He was 21 years old, just graduated in cybersecurity, and only had a few months of work experience in a helpdesk – not a security role. This in a market that wants 5 years of experience to do the most mundane tasks.

The lack of experience meant the bulk of his CV were his grades, and they weren't impressive.

To the contrary: they were poor, barely passing. But they were *consistently* poor.

I had a suspicion they were the grades of someone that was bored, doing the minimum to get by, and I told him to come in for a chat.

He came up to Salford, from Wrexham, and was not only bright, but engaging, able to communicate, look you in the eye, liked to experiment at home, and even knew who Les Brown was.

Now a 21-year-old who knows a great motivational speaker like that has to be someone who believes in human potential and his own.

Now, at this point we had no security budget and no real tooling. We did however have comprehensive MS 365 licensing which meant we could use Defender ATP, Sentinel, and other tools in the offering.

The thing is he'd never heard of any of these, but I didn't think that was a problem. I'd just find a few books and drop them on his desk on week one.

It turns out that Microsoft doesn't really produce much in the way of literature around these solutions. Whoops.

By the time I went to him with a few articles he could get started on, he was already neck-deep in dozens of knowledge articles and webinars and asking about enabling and connecting features we didn't even know existed. I was as new to MS's offering as he was and now rely on him to make sure we get the most out of it.

No one would hire him due to the lack of experience in general, not to mention that he knew nothing about the tooling that would be a core part of his job. But within a week he was helping to define how *we* would use that tooling.

On to my second hire at UoS…

I needed to be able to refocus on the strategy, I was getting too busy staying on top of things. I needed a hand with business discovery and less technical daily activities so I could put more times towards defining strategy and process (my framework) and gaining support from the top.

I'm often contacted by recruiters after hiring someone, with them asking where I found them. This is particularly fun with this hire because I get to answer "In a bar."

I was in a Manchester bar where a local DevSecOps event finished. Several geeks (I say this affectionately, no need to call the offended police) started filling the place up.

Here they were, probably a dozen of them, talking about code and security and DevOps, all in that awkward excited way only true geeks can pull off.

Except one guy. He was also talking the talk but was less *technical* in how he spoke. He was saying the same things but was somehow less "geeky."

He also spoke very calmly, and in a genuinely inquisitive manner. And not just to the geeks either, but to anyone and everyone in that bar. He could talk to the geeks, the bar tender, the suits at the next table, random people, and dare I say it, even to the girls (gasp!). He was very easy going about it, approaching people and engaging them in conversation without hesitation and with genuine enthusiasm and curiosity, and *they* happily engaged with him as a result.

We connected on LinkedIn and talked for a little while. He was in his 40's, ex-forces, worked as a helicopter technician, then spent several years caring for family and operating their bed and breakfast. Before all that, he'd bounced all over the world for years.

He liked to tinker with tech and wound up on this DevSecOps course even though he'd never really worked in IT. His only security exposure was some playing around with DevOps and some Splunk time.

The few technical skills he had I didn't even want.

But, a recurring theme in this book is the importance of engaging business stakeholders. To find out what's going on, to build relationships, to know what we need to protect.

For that, this guy was 24k gold. Naturally *very* curious, great with people, and detail oriented to boot. Even if he didn't understand something he'd ask the right questions, and sometimes he'd even ask a question someone more experienced, with a bit more tunnel vision, wouldn't think of.

He also genuinely wanted to fix things once he understood the problem and didn't limit his thinking to specific areas or functions, which means his solutions tend to be more common sense, further upstream, and cover more issues than just the one that sparked the thought.

I wrote up a job spec specifically for him, around his strengths, had HR post it, and gave him the link to apply.

By the way, I do this last bit for everyone. In an age where we're supposedly celebrating individuals and diversity, we sure seem to be trying hard to not consider what makes people individuals and how they can uniquely contribute by dumbing things down to a few "I know or have done this particular little thing" tick-boxes.

I much prefer finding out what a person can bring, as an individual, leveraging their full abilities and potential, and also the areas they want to grow into and building a job spec around that. I genuinely think we're doing this backwards.

Say we have 26 requirements, A to Z, we then look for one person that can do A & B, another that can do C & D, another that can do E & F, another that can do G & H, and so on. Because this is how the industry has structured roles. An analyst, an engineer, an architect, a consultant, a manager, an auditor, etc.

Meanwhile you have someone that can do A, C, E, H, J, P, R, T, V, X & Z and they get overlooked because they don't fit the job description of doing just A & B, or just C & D. It's ridiculous.

Find good people, from a human perspective, then work out what they can do, how to make them fit together, and build your job specs around them, structure your team, organisation, responsibilities, and operations around those people.

Yet one more way to get far more output than people think is possible out of a team of a given size.

You have multiple locations and want to commoditise all roles so you can mirror everything? No two teams are the same anyway, no two individuals are the same. Don't be lazy and do what you can to maximize each teams' potential.

But what about role redundancy and cross coverage? With a good culture, solid curious people will naturally learn what each other are doing, as they should in order to make sure all the pieces fit. It also means they're often cross-training without you needing to lift a finger.

I want to close this by saying that when I was still job-hunting for a CISO role, one common road block with HR and hiring managers was that they wanted someone who was a "strong manager" (when they didn't just want a box-ticker). That sounds perfectly reasonable, except they believe that means someone who can "manage" a team of 50 people. My question is, between someone who can manage 50 people to get the job done, and someone who can get the same job done with 10 people by unlocking their potential and leveraging a better approach, who's the better manager?

I'd argue the latter but unfortunately being good at something in a new way often means getting filtered out by outdated status quo ideas and criteria. I keep building smaller yet more productive teams as I develop as a manager/leader, and this has ironically made it increasingly harder to find work.

It's just one more challenge for me to overcome and once again highlights the importance of networking and reputation, but I also want to caution others to not filter out the best people by looking for the wrong thing or relying on the status quo.

Be open to new approaches and ideas, consider the complete context, and hire yourself some fantastic potential.

They don't fit the mould? Break it.

What the Hell Is a Unicorn?

I hear a lot about "unicorn hunting", job specs with unrealistic requirements wanting half a dozen certifications and years of experience in something that appeared 6 months ago.

My question is: What the hell is a unicorn?

I don't feel that someone that has a CISSP, CISA, CISM, CEH, OSCP, etc., is a unicorn. Hell, it's more likely they're heavily indoctrinated, not flexible, and probably not what you need anyway.

I find it strange that this is what people think a unicorn is, that people are chasing something rare that's not even what they need.

To me the real unicorn is something else. Attitude and aptitude, drive, potential. That's the starting point to *making* a unicorn. A real unicorn is someone that has those properties and is then moulded to your organisation, who grows into it, fitting it perfectly. A person that has been nurtured into a role, who therefore, in addition to having a perfectly fitted skillset, cares about their function, their organization, and their contribution to it.

The other thing to note is that the requirements can change dramatically when you shift to a more proactive approach.

To go back to the car factory analogy (again…), I quite like people that are new to the industry, because they're more likely to be the guys standing at the fence thinking it's ridiculous that the cars are coming out of the factory from the 3rd floor and landing into the lot all mangled.

They still use common sense rather than "industry thinking", whereas if I hired an experienced InfoSec person for twice the money they'd likely just perpetuate the same old status quo, making a beeline for that parking lot and start fixing cars.

Then there are the detractors telling me the InfoSec equivalent of "We repair 1,000 radiators a day and your guy has never done one! How can they be qualified to do this job?!" to which I reply "My guy doesn't *need* to change radiators, ever, because he'll fix the assembly line so they don't get damaged in the first place."

Yes, he/she is going to learn what a radiator install looks like, but only to make sure the entire build process (the root cause he/she will fix with common sense) is solid and resilient so that all the repair work is eliminated. If one ever *really* needs fixing, they'll figure it out anyway.

Unicorns are grown, and they probably look a lot different than most people think. They're also quite rewarding to grow. Get farming.

Tool Jockeys

No, we're not hiring the real unicorns, but we are hiring a lot of tool jockeys.

If you're hiring *primarily* based on needing people to operate specific tools, versus needing people to *help the business*, I'd argue that your hiring is significantly flawed.

Possibly your entire approach to information security is flawed.

The most important thing when looking to hire people is to find talent and human potential rather than any static skill.

Those properties will grant far more ability to *solve problems* in all kinds of ways, versus just mindlessly performing never-ending operational tasks.

To be a good leader, a good boss, you must be able to recognise these.

Thinking, initiative, fresh ideas. These are the critical outputs you want from staff. Operational roles can and should be largely automated.

Now when I said operational roles just there I am talking about those operational roles that remain once you implement a proactive approach. An analyst-type person should not be dealing with similar incidents and opening tickets, but rather spotting an issue, ask why, pull on the strings until the *true* root cause is found, and address that issue, once.

This kind of thinking won't map to any particular tool but will boost your environment's integrity and the level of assurance that it can provide by a greater level than any reactive security tooling could possibly muster.

It's what you should look for, focus on. The best part? It doesn't even require much experience and is easy to mentor.

It's important to get this kind of thinking into your more junior staff and functions. While these individuals tend to be relegated to menial work, they are often the closest to the ground where you will be spending less time and they must be mentally equipped to spot and solve, or at least report issues that have true root causes further upstream.

This way you can action them, whether that be immediately or by bringing them into your strategic plans. Tool jockeys without initiative and curiosity will miss these, you will have blind spots, and the integrity of your estate will start eroding without ever being noticed, until it's too late.

Hiring Fresh

Continuing on from the skills gap, it's interesting that everyone is raving that we need more new people in the industry, but then no one wants to hire them. It seems resources with less than 5 years' experience (and some with much more) and numerous certs (some of which have experience as a prerequisite) can't find work.

Now let me be very straight here: there is no skills gap, and the reason companies (read: hiring InfoSec managers!) are asking for most certifications and years of experience is that they probably don't know what they need to do and think they're playing it safe by only hiring experienced candidates.

The problem is that when you're an organisation that doesn't even know what it's doing in terms of building a functioning InfoSec apparatus and your hiring baseline is X years on the job and certifications, you end up with indoctrinated resources just as ineffective as the people hiring them.

And, as I'll discuss more later, indoctrination of a broken approach (which doesn't work, but that we keep trying to scale up thinking it eventually will, thus creating a "skills shortage") is one of the biggest problems standing in the way of effective InfoSec today.

If I had to build a cutting-edge security organisation with maximum performance in mind I'd start from scratch. I'd hire fresh graduates and people with minimal experience.

Even promising kids with no experience. If it was an extraordinarily large or distributed organisation I might also hire a couple of the more open-minded senior people in the field. For context, we're currently managing a 30,000-user organisation with a team of 2 junior people and myself without too much trouble because we focus on the upstream issues and process rather than fighting fires, so chances are one decent leader can build a solid team out of only juniors. The secret is that they don't stay junior for long if you do your job right.

Let me tell you that 4 years of college, in my book, is what you'll learn in 3 months on the job if you're driven and/or have the right mentor. That, and much more.

So, this team of grads and people with minimal experience... I wouldn't teach them "how to do security" like a CISSP course book. I'd show them how information security doesn't work. Broken enterprise applications, change management processes introducing vulnerabilities, poor system builds, missing patches, obvious vulnerabilities, misconfigured or incompletely installed tools, etc. all despite countless controls in place.

And I'd ask them to sort out *why* these things were happening, why no one was addressing poor processes, why people complain about legacy systems but never bother creating standards for their replacements and keep ending up in the same boat. I'd make them think about the situation and how/why it came to be, not chase the endless individual issues that result.

I'd then show them how to follow those whys and how to prevent those issues from even coming into existence. Teach them to be multidisciplinary, to deal with people, to argue, to engage, to nurture relationships that breed collaboration. Enable them to eliminate root causes, and the very existence of the issues most InfoSec teams spend 90% of their time hopelessly running after.

These are the real skills they need (make sure to also nurture them through everything from sitting in a board meeting, tagging along on audits, vendor meetings, how to ask for a raise, etc.) and there are many 5, even 10+ year industry veterans that don't have them. They're skills they won't learn in school. But more tragically they're skills they won't learn on the job in most places either.

Why? Because we've come full circle to the lack of leadership and human engagement, and the failure to understand that it's the needed foundation for an effective security organisation.

The funny part? As I mentioned in the Unicorn chapter, even as blank canvases they can often be more valuable than more "experienced" and expensive resources. In the case of the car factory analogy, an expensive industry-indoctrinated resource will rush into the parking lot and apply great technical skills to start changing radiators and body panels. A complete neophyte with no idea how to do that will instead stand there, find the fact that we're lobbing cars from the 3rd floor very odd indeed, and use basic common sense to overcome that problem. A far bigger problem.

So, go on, hire your hard to find, expensive, low-value (let's be honest, we're looking at filling roles, not value), indoctrinated industry drones that fit your pigeonholes. Some of us are happy to invest in fresh people and turn them into superstars that make a difference.

Equality and Diversity

No two human beings are equal. Everyone is an individual. Equal rights and *consideration* is all we can hope for.

Note that I said equal consideration, not opportunity. There's a reason for that.

How do you measure opportunity? I have more opportunities now than I would otherwise have at this point in my life precisely because of the struggles I endured; tricky childhood, manic depressive mother, teenage fatherhood, High School dropout, awful bosses, bouts of homelessness, and depression.

Many of the best, strongest, and toughest people I know are the ones that have had no choice but to overcome obstacles and grown and gained grit and determination in spades as a result. I believe in helping, supporting, and mentoring people, but not in coddling them in such a way that prevents them from realising their full potential. There is a thin line between the two that I feel we are crossing all too often.

After that initial consideration of someone's *potential*, everything should be down to the individual. It's your job to consider that individual free of biases.

Take the time to get to know them, see that potential, and help them achieve it. That's your job.

Please support people as individuals, not labels. That is all I want to say about this subject.

If you are one of those people, with those challenges, stop making excuses, stop blaming others, and focus. Use that adversity because it may just be your biggest blessing.

Personal tip, go out on YouTube and go give Les Brown a listen. I hope you love it. *You gotta be hungry.*

Certifications

A word about certifications, taken from a LinkedIn article I published back in 2018.

10 years ago, my email signature looked somewhat like this:

Greg van der Gaast, CISSP, ISSAP, ISSMP, ISSEP, CISA, CISM, CGEIT, CEH, MCP (3X), CCNA, CCDA, CCNP, CCDP, CCNA WAN, CCNP WAN, CCDP WAN, MCNS, ITILv3, PMP.

Today it reads:

Greg van der Gaast

Why? Well for one I've let every single one of those certifications expire.

Potential employers and recruiters balk at this. "Ah, he doesn't have any certifications."

But not a single one of them can explain to me how my not paying renewal fees somehow reduces my ability to actually perform the work. Sure, you could argue that a certification means you know something, but it boggles the mind that hiring managers seem to think you un-know everything the certification stands for when it expires.

Does ISACA or (ISC)2 come to your home in the middle of the night and lobotomise the part of your brain with that knowledge because you haven't paid up?

Yet this plays a significant role in the selection and rejection of potential personnel. It is warping the way we judge candidates' fitness for Information Security roles. Or other roles for that matter, since the same applies to non-InfoSec certifications.

First, we value a candidate because he/she has a piece of paper saying they passed a test demonstrating a certain knowledge, and then we dismiss the supposedly valued candidate because the commercial entity behind that piece of paper hasn't been paid lately.

I find it absolutely baffling.

Then we come to the second reason my certifications are expired: The relevance of the certifications themselves.

When just starting out, the academic and theoretical knowledge learned in the process of obtaining these certifications can be invaluable. You learn the lingo, some concepts, and signal that you have certain abilities even though you haven't yet been able to demonstrate them with your limited work experience.

But if you've been doing Information Security seriously for any amount of time, barring you've just branched into a new area, then you've hopefully outgrown these certifications. Personally, when I go back to review them with my accumulated experience, I struggle.

I recently picked up the latest CISSP course prep. Everything discussed is at a rather basic and oversimplified level compared to my personal level of know-how and *reality*. I'd say it doesn't even mention 95% of the InfoSec sphere. Worse though, is the fact that a lot of it is wrong. In some cases, it's even technically incorrect, but in *many* cases what it preaches in terms of approach is really to be avoided.

When I have to set aside what experience has taught me and memorise which wrong answers the certification authority expects me to put down during the test, that is a certification that is not worth my time. It is a certification that, from a professional ethics standpoint, I do not want to be associated with.

Maybe that's harsh, because as I said before, there is value in these certifications, especially when starting out. What concerns me is people identifying themselves according to those certifications (as I once did), doggedly sticking to their teachings, and not outgrowing them. I feel in many cases people are letting it define them in their roles and their careers as Information Security professionals. That is bad.

Let me use an analogy:

The best drivers are often those that understand the reasoning behind the rules, explore a bit beyond them, and are able to apply, bend, or even disregard them for the given situation. 9 days out of 10 it may be hard to see the difference between the bad/basic drivers and the good ones.

But on day 10, one will blindly smash into a truck that just pulled out in front of them at 70mph because they never developed more advanced driving skills by going beyond the limits of the curriculum. Plus, they *couldn't* avoid it because they strictly follow the rules and you're not allowed to change lanes here anyway because of the solid yellow lines.

The other will have the wherewithal, skills, experience, and, possibly most important of all, the needed *disregard* for that solid yellow lane divider to swerve well out of the lane and avoid becoming a pancake.

We've all had to learn a curriculum and take a practical test to get our driving licenses. It was written to be as simple and generic as possible, so that virtually anyone could pass it. During this test we had to respect all the rules, and those arbitrary lines painted on the tarmac. We learned a lot, and it was beneficial to us. But if 10 years on you're still driving like you did on your test that day, and you still think everything in that basic oversimplified curriculum is the best way of doing things, chances are you're a *terrible* driver.

Less scrupulous people will carve you up, you're not going to win any races, and sooner or later you're going to be unable to avoid slamming into a truck. Annoyingly, you're also going to be in the good drivers' way most of the time too. Bogging things down, creating traffic, and, ironically, increasing the likelihood of accidents.

And make no mistake, InfoSec is a race against unscrupulous people. Some of them drive big trucks.

All of this is actually a symptom of a bigger problem. Indoctrination. Cue our next chapter.

Indoctrination

We do things a certain way in Information Security. But are we sure it's the right way?

I'm not, but it's incredibly hard to break through indoctrination.

People keep going back to what they know, and it becomes self-reinforcing. The fact that Information Security is something abstract to many people, something you can't see or touch, can make it harder still because it rarely gets questioned by outsiders.

One of the best ways to defeat indoctrination is to present an equivalent thought or concept in an area that's more likely to be governed by common sense.

Here is the analogy I like to use to explain the indoctrination of InfoSec's reactive/SecOps approach.

Imagine you had a car that went one mile on a gallon of fuel. Already you're thinking that's terrible mileage, there's something wrong with it. Let's pop the hood/bonnet and have a look, right? That's rational objective thinking.

Now imagine *all* cars got one mile per gallon. Imagine all cars, *for as far back as you can remember*, got one mile per gallon. It would now seem perfectly normal to you. You wouldn't even think of having a look at the engine.

Instead, you'd probably be thinking about filling up right about now.

A whole industry would likely grow around fuelling cars; faster pumps, fuelling stations would appear every other mile on the motorway, maybe we'd develop drones to fill up our cars while we were on the move! Wouldn't that be amazing? This industry would become massive, employ millions of people, help drive the economy, and would not spend any time looking at the *why* we were only getting 1mpg.

In fact, they'd think you were crazy for doing so. If you did figure out why, most people wouldn't even listen to you, because you're clearly a crazy person. Some people might realise you were onto something, and they may feel quite threatened by it and even try to silence you because of the threat to the establishment or even their livelihood.

This is how reactive information security works today. SecOps catching issues caused primarily by poor hygiene and process further upstream, and no one seems to want to fix it, in fact most of us think it's perfectly normal.

Think about it.

Standardisation

As we just mentioned, people in Information Security are getting alarmingly indoctrinated. I feel some of this is due to *standardisation*.

More and more organisations are trying to standardise concepts, approaches, technologies, training, knowledge. ISACA, COBIT, ISO, NIST, Prince2, Agile, ITIL are all examples of this. Someone creates a model and people bind themselves to it.

We are losing the ability to look into details and formulate our own conclusions. Very few people pick apart each approach and take away only what works for them, very few people criticise.

Even with technologies, we rarely discuss the detailed mechanics of specific solutions, instead broadly categorising and labelling them with an acronym or buzzword, or both. This stops us from looking at the details, where we may find synergies, or concerns. I've seen phenomenal technologies with huge value fail because the market wouldn't consider them, because they didn't fit a particular label.

We are turning ourselves into drones. And we reward drones while people that use objective thinking, people that see that there is more to it than just definitions, are often dismissed.

I saw a post on LinkedIn once saying that, including various factors, we would spend a trillion dollars on Information Security in the coming years. A trillion! $1,000,000,000,000.

That's a thousand times a thousand million dollars. It is more than the gross GDP of the Netherlands, the 17th largest economy in the world.

The same article said total losses to all forms of cybercrime are estimated to reach 5 to 6 trillion.

That is more than the GDP of Japan, the third largest economy in the world. More than the combined income of one hundred and thirty million people in one of the most developed countries in the world.

It is more than twice the GDP of the entire African continent.

The Information Security sector is about as effective at stopping cybercrime as stern words are at stopping Mexican drug cartels.

Think about it. Security professionals probably outnumber hackers by 1,000 to 1. We're probably spending £10,000 for every £1 hackers spend. We're on the wrong side for any value for money here.

Every year Information Security spending increases by X, and losses to cybercrime increase by (X)2. The delta is growing exponentially, and indoctrination is one of the main fundamental causes.

Do we really think this is sustainable?

We are creating an army of drones. Drones doing operations, drones doing coding, drones doing engineering, drones doing architecture, drones doing compliance, drones doing management.

All this to go up against malicious hackers. Hackers, a byword for ingenious out of the box thinking. People that thrive precisely on breaking systems, taking advantage of structure, and exploiting the status quo by out-thinking it.

Here we are, making it easier for them, in many ways discouraging open thinking in the very people supposed to head them off. HR, recruiters, and hiring managers often penalising those that don't subscribe to the indoctrination, rewarding those that do.

How much more down the wrong path could we be going?

When I'm asked for specific details about how I'm going to implement an information security strategy at a company, my answer is usually "I'll tell you in 2-3 weeks." Because while I may be experienced and exceptionally quick at picking up on things, I still can't tell you until I see your exact situation, talk to people, and have a really good think. And even then, that approach will morph and change as I discover new things.

Information Security is not just a knowledge game, it is primarily a *thinking* game. The knowledge is a consequence. If you're obtaining it without thinking, it's probably not the right knowledge.

Anyone that has a canned answer with a bunch of methodology and technology buzzwords isn't going to make a dent in your fundamental security issues. Sure their reports might look great, but is that really what you want?

We need more thinkers, more true leaders, more people who won't limit themselves to industry concepts. People able to mentally match and hopefully outmanoeuvre the threat.

We need to teach Information Security personnel to be less bound by structure, and use more open-ended thinking, to never stop questioning... everything.

If there's anything we should be pushing ourselves to do it's to stop limiting ourselves with academic definitions, market standards, and industry trends. Be more like hackers.

Do what you need for your business. Think it through every step of the way, without paying mind to these external influences, and you'll end up with solutions so efficient, so cost-effective, and so tightly and perfectly suited to your specific organisation that attackers won't be able to find a gap to pry on.

Intuition

Be more Intuitive. Take a moment and drop what you think you know and the formalised methods in which things should supposedly be done.

You may just find that, for you, or for your organisation (once you've learned how it works), there is a better way.

Allow yourself to feel your way through things, even in a discipline as technical as security.

I've been able to predict how likely organisations were to get breached by picking up signs that had nothing to do with tech and to do so with amazing accuracy.

I once wrote an article about a CISO's misandrist attitude. She generalised all "white men" as entitled and bad, showing closed-mindedness, and, ironically, arrogance and entitlement on her part. I said it was the kind of thinking that would lead to breaches, because she showed strong bias and an unwillingness to consider individual situations; details.

Ridiculous? The company she worked for, a large insurer, announced a data breach less than a month later.

Not only will intuition help you spot things missed by siloes and frameworks and best practices, it'll give you a feeling for things even when you don't have hard data.

Be more Intuitive. It is immensely powerful.

Language

Touching on indoctrination before, remember that language shapes and also *limits* our thinking. When we start using industry terms, we limit our thinking.

We even use plain English words within a very specific scope which means we can no longer use them in their broader English sense which would have led us to reflect upon them more deeply, instead we immediately jump to indoctrinated conclusions and associations now tied to those words instead of thinking them through.

The word "compliance" for example is extremely broad, and yet we immediately associate it to compliance to external standards such as ISO 27001 and NIST when in reality it means so much more than that. I struggle to explain compliance to internal standards because I can no longer use the word "compliance" for its true meaning!

Always think whether you could explain what you're saying to a 5-year-old, but also always think of the 5-year-old's perspective. Would this make any sense to me if I was the 5-year-old? And would the 5-year-old make me realise something? For example, that "compliance" doesn't necessarily mean to some 3rd party standard, since the child wouldn't know about it and therefore not assume!

Once again, "If you can't explain it in plain language, you don't understand it well enough."

If you're relying on artificial language to be understood, then you are in an indoctrination bubble and need to get out. This is critical because while we may think we're making sense, we're actually spewing out industry jargon that has connotations for us, but is far less tangible to others, and sometimes to reality.

Be careful.

Bonus Round

I mentioned at the beginning of this book that I would focus on proactive security concepts and that I would leave building a framework and strategic engagement for a future book.

We have touched a bit on engagement on this book. Enough to start you thinking.

We haven't however gone into much detail on how to structure a bespoke framework.

While I plan on producing on entire book on the subject, I didn't want to leave you without at least a starting point on how I approach that. Therefore, I'm throwing in a few more chapters in the hope of providing some insights.

Here goes.

Why a Framework?

Security Operations, whether done by InfoSec or IT, tend to be a mess.

As we've discussed, they should be delivering a foundation of integrity onto which we can build, but they rarely if ever do, and it is the reason behind so many failures.

Here are some of the key ones I see on this front:

- A lack of general organisation.
- A tick-box implementation without further consideration.
- No clear definition of activities.
- Impossibility to consistently enforce processes.
- Lack of detail in processes and policies.
- Loose pieces of documentation. (Policies, processes, standards, etc.)
- A lack of systematic holistic approach in documenting operations.
- Leaving many IT processes with heavy security impacts up to IT with no review of their efficacy.
- Processes not well aligned to each other.
- Process/work duplication due to a lack of integration.
- Process outputs not feeding into other processes and processes and registries consequently going out of sync.

- References to documents and policies no one can locate because they weren't considered and updated in conjunction with the documents referencing them.
- Documents often out of date.
- Documents in conflict with each other (even if in small ways) because they come from different sources or were written under different contexts without considering the big picture.
- Much, much, more.

As a result, here were my realisations when I first put thought into organising security in a large multi-site organisation:

We need all Security processes and standards, as well as any IT processes and standards that have impact on security, well documented.

Documentation must be highly prescriptive. Anyone should be able to execute the process without needing to look elsewhere (or, when they do, the location of the external documentation must also be indicated and it shout be equally prescriptive).

We need a container where all security *and security-relevant* (IT and business processes are kept. Not just a storage location but an organised structure where an overview identifies every single component. *Nothing* lives outside this structure.

We need a framework.

Building a Framework

There are many frameworks used for InfoSec out there. NIST, ISO 27001, MITRE, COBIT, SOC2, etc.

I've already written about how I feel it's a better-fitting and more sustainable approach to craft a bespoke framework for your organisation (in terms of maintaining integrity rather than putting effort towards framework upkeep). It ensures tighter alignment and fit and doesn't expose us to the risks of interpretative and priority bias that 3rd party frameworks tend to introduce. Just the thought exercise in how to structure things for *ourselves* can be extremely productive. Mapping those external standards back to our framework for 3rd party compliance reasons can then be done quite easily afterwards.

But what should such a framework look like? Heck, what *is* a framework?

I like to keep it simple and essentially consider it a container in which we put the elements needed to establish and run a successful operational programme. Like a box or wireframe where we can put things in.

Of course, when we say "framework" we also mean those components within the box. So, what are those components?

Procedures, standards, policies, processes, etc. We relate to them as documents. We have to be very careful to not think that they are *just* documents though. They are not.

215

They are actions, operations, and rules. But they do have to be documented, and that means documents.

So, our framework is a collection of documents (which must be actioned). Making sure those documents get actioned and actioned properly is a big part of the framework's purpose. Its structure is important.

I have yet to see a single Information Security organisation effectively manage documents. In 20 years of doing this, not one could provide an exhaustive listing of all InfoSec operational and process documents when asked, or maintain them up to date, or approved. Document management system or not.

It's a nightmare. If we're going to prescriptively define and enforce Information Security, the very first thing we have to do is manage the documentation that embodies it.

What are the usual problems? Well, "reactive security" is one. In short: We discovered a need, because of audit/compliance or some other reason, and we created a policy or process for it to check that tick-box. It doesn't get used much, and it ends up rotting in a drawer, forgotten.

Every time someone's told me they had this covered I inevitably found they were wrong. What they actually had was documents that were disorganised, not linked together, clearly not thought out holistically or according to their reality on the ground, often not formatted consistently, were out of date, and often unknown to the very people that were supposed to implement the processes described.

Setting aside the quality of the documents, it also took me longer than it should have to get access to them.

How auditors don't find this alarming is beyond me. If it takes that long to pull a process or system snapshot, how can they possibly be securing anything effectively?

Two things need to happen.

Firstly, we need to reduce the number of documents by thinking through what we actually need, and how (and why) we actually use and implement the various procedures and processes. How do we do that? Just like we said before; we get down into the weeds and talk to the troops. Observe, ask questions, work out all the interactions between processes, people, teams, groups, how it goes up the chain of command, and *validate every step of the way with the people actually doing the work.* Practical areas like standards around email, removable media, patching, or systems provisioning, for example.

Secondly, we need a proper practical framework. By "practical" I mean practical for us. A framework that defines and lists every single document we need. A self-contained framework that all rules, guidelines, standards, processes, and procedures live within. So that when you are looking at the documentation stack of the framework, you have everything in your hands, nothing happens outside of it. Nothing gets lost, nothing escapes renewal, nothing escapes the built-in continuous improvement processes that are also part of such a framework.

That's right, instead of running around for a month before an audit, trying to round up and update documents, you just hand the auditor your framework's documentation stack and send them on their way.

I've had management teams freak out when they found out I wasn't preparing for impending ISO27001 and PCI audits. "What preparation? I'm just going to open all the cupboards for them and leave them to it."

In one case the auditing team was perplexed, only to follow up with an email that complimented the approach and said they only needed the required minimum evidence as a formality because it was clear from how prescriptive and current the framework was that everything was being done. In another case the auditor's feedback got me skipping a couple of levels in the org chart and reporting to the board.

Here's a practical example of how I like to organise security documentation. It's the framework I put together for the University of Salford (which will see more tweaks as it develops):

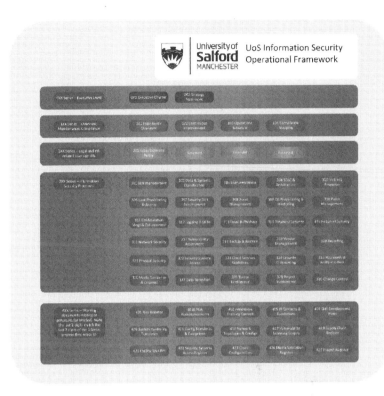

You'll see the following elements I usually include in a framework:

- The Executive Charter (covered in the next chapter of this book).
- Strategy statements on how we will cost-effectively gain traction, resource, achieve overall objectives.
- An overview of the programme (the security organisation, perspective, scopes, the documentation set, and more)
- A document management/continuous improvement process. (Yes, I run my own

document management system, naming conventions, etc., for my department. Most companies' systems are either not fit for purpose full stop or not conducive to how I want to structure things.)

- An operations schedule.
- Mapping documents showing how we meet 3rd party requirements.
- Any legal, consent, user policy, or data protection documentation.
- The multitude of individual policies, processes, and standards around all parts of IT/Security/Business. (By the way, there's no real reason you can't put them all in a single document covering an area when you have top to bottom engagement and visibility. "But we've always done it this way." is not a reason.)
- Any working documents needed to support the various processes.

Note also that the framework is organised into several levels or layers:

- Executive.
- Framework Overview/Maintenance/Compliance.
- Legal, regional, and user consent considerations (things like privacy policies, AUP's and DPIAs).
- The operational processes, procedures/guidelines.
- Working documents.

But it's not just about containing the documents. The structure, content, and purpose of those individual documents matters. As does how they relate to each other.

Note: While this is something for the future book, *Structuring InfoSec*, which will focus more on structuring and organising InfoSec activities, I do want to at least mention the importance of processes being self-healing and self-checking, as well as cross-reinforcing to minimise the possibilities of things falling through the cracks and picking them up when they do.

It's important to note that while each document/process looks like a standalone brick, every single one is written with all the others in mind and most of the "bricks" have inputs from and output to other the bricks (processes/documents), reinforcing each other, staying in sync, and eliminating some duplication at the same time.

A perfect example is one we so often see: different asset counts depending on who you ask; Anti-Virus, Asset Management, and Patch management tools/teams all reporting different numbers.

Why are all these processes being applied to different numbers of hosts? Why are there asset counts/registers for each? Clearly it should be unified. It's not only duplicate effort, but it's also highlighting inconsistencies: proof that there are gaps.

Instead, the Asset Management process should feed into those processes, just like the Joiners/Leavers/Movers process should tap into the Asset Management process and so on and so forth. They should all be linked together, and you should have processes doing the odd bit of cross checking whenever you see the opportunity for one process to validate or reinforce another.

Let me finish by saying that this is how I do things and, for me, with my proactive approach, it works far better at delivering consistent assurance throughout an organisation than any other method I have seen to date. But, as I've mentioned before, the last thing you should do is follow me blindly. I want people to think and question.

While I adapt the scope of individual components, their composition, and the structure of my frameworks to some degree (sometimes extensively) for every environment, there may be a completely different way of doing things that no one's thought of yet.

The Executive Charter

As I mentioned in the previous chapter, many things about a framework should be adapted for a given environment. The executive charter is no different. In fact, it's likely the most crucial.

That said, it is always present, and it has a very important job. So important that, despite being only a few pages long, you should spend weeks getting a feel for your organisation before starting, and not be afraid of spending hours finessing its contents.

This document goes to the board and must support your framework (by addressing every fundamental problem area you might anticipate) before you start building it out.

You may not get another chance.

In my frameworks this document sits at the very top. It is the least prescriptive of all the documents but provides the authorisation and authority for all the layers below it.

You cannot implement a working information security programme without significant management buy-in, without a mandate.

For the board it's more than signing a document, it's the confirmation of their support and involvement. If you can't get management past this stage, either figure out how or get another job.

It has to be understood that Information Security is the responsibility of the CEO and the board. It is a job they are not qualified to do and must delegate accordingly. With that delegation they must pass not just responsibility, but also the required authority.

It is my responsibility to take my car to the shop for repairs if I can't do them myself. If my *trusted* mechanic tells me he needs me to authorise working on the car how he sees fit and that it will cost X, then I need to give him X and the authority to take apart and do whatever he needs to get the job done. If I didn't pay him (resources) or didn't authorise him to touch certain parts of the car (authority), then it's not his fault if my car isn't running at the end of the day, it's mine.

I typically make about 10 statements, which I call directives, in an executive charter:

1. **Overall Responsibility**. We state that senior management accepts overall responsibility for Information Security.

2. **Mandate**. We state that management delegates the above responsibility to the Information Security organisation, and clearly state the mission for which that

organisation is receiving this responsibility (InfoSec mission statement). This is also a good place to mention that you will report to them and how often (don't be greedy).

3. **Define Security Strategy.** How will InfoSec deliver? This is where we state that we will create and deliver an operational Information Security framework that will develop, disseminate, and enforce a cohesive set of processes and procedures as well as implementing technological elements as needed.

4. **Authority.** Here we state that management grants InfoSec the necessary authority to apply and enforce all elements of the framework. Some organisations may have competing authorities, this is a good place to define hierarchies/priorities.

5. **Resources & Support.** Here we clearly state that senior management shall provide all reasonable necessary resources for the implementation of the above framework. It also seeks formal support from the board in the form of recurring security meetings at board level for you to brief them, and their public support of the programme being communicated to the wider organisation.

6. **Project Involvement.** I like to mention this one specifically because it's important to drive it through. We must be involved at the initial stages in order to deliver a solid security foundation, so let's state that management will instruct all project leaders to involve InfoSec from initiation. To avoid any issues with non-compliance to

this, management shall give explicit authority for InfoSec to request details on any aspect of any project at any time. InfoSec shall also be involved in any executive or technology roadmaps and be able to impose any security gates it sees fit on projects. Finally, InfoSec shall have a final say on project go-lives.

7. **Control Over Change.** Pretty much the same as above, but for any operational changes. We must be able to review and approve/deny changes.

8. **Security Exceptions.** Here we state that we, InfoSec, can be overruled. Let's face it, some people will always try to go over our heads. Sometimes some people are just jerks, but even the most security savvy businesses can have a business need to override InfoSec standards and processes now and again. It's important that we account/allow for it and make sure it's done through a formal risk accountability process. This adds not just accountability, but also predictability to exceptions. If we don't set a clear path for these exceptions, they end up all over the place, unmanageable, and often undocumented.

9. **Visibility.** Here we state that InfoSec can request any information about existing or new infrastructure, projects, applications, etc. This is essential to the application of InfoSec and the proactive discovery of issues. We can now proactively investigate anything we have a hunch about, not just the new stuff rolling in. I also like to present the concept of "Direct Visibility" here,

meaning we must be able to *directly* see the systems in the environment, without being dependent on IT.

10. **Daily Operations**. This is where we define who has responsibility for daily operations. In some organisations there are dedicated InfoSec resources for everything, others delegate to regular IT staff, others outsource. This is where we define that, and the stakeholders responsible will be added to the charter's approving signatories.

Once again, do feel free to modify any of these. Split them, remove some, add more, whatever it takes to best cover the underlying challenges you anticipate in *your* particular organisation. This is why it's so important to take the time to first get to know the organisation as thoroughly as possible before creating your charter.

Many of these directives are in place to make our future framework/programme functions properly. Only once you have a good idea of what your strategy is and what organisational, technical, cultural, and political problems you will face will you be able to write the executive charter that will make success possible.

Allow me to go a bit further into detail, to show you how I format things, to give you a better understanding.

Remember that the charter should do everything we need it to do, but also be brief.

When I write anything for senior management, especially when it's a new proposal that they're not actively expecting, I tend to write, rewrite, and rewrite some more. Then keep the best 10% and throw out the rest. This is an audience whose time you must be mindful of.

All too often senior InfoSec professionals fall into 2 categories: The technical ones, and the more "managerial" or "GRC" type guys (and gals).

Board members do not tend to be technical, certainly not InfoSec technical, and no one wants to invite the techie over for dinner, so spare them.

What most people don't realise is that the "managerial/GRC" type is also very capable of causing plenty of eye rolling among the boardroom crowd. The former often spout a bunch of industry gobbledygook that means nothing to the latter.

If we can't properly address and connect with senior management (who are both tech *and* IT GRC laymen), we've already lost. We're basically demonstrating that we live in a bubble rather than in the business, and we're going to struggle to win executive support if we don't come across as all about the business

These soft skills must be mastered for effective InfoSec management, so here are some pointers on how and why I structure an executive charter the way I do.

My executive charters tend to be about 4 pages long:

Page 1:

Any document should start with an introduction. These are typically obvious and just 1-2 paragraphs. Everything must be leveraged for maximum impact, so I state not just that this is an Information Security Executive Charter (note the capitals when addressing the document itself) aimed at defining the approach and backing for an overall information security strategy, but also that it is part of a larger framework. I then include a colourful diagram of the framework.

We must right away convey that this is not just another InfoSec document to fill drawers with, that it is part of something larger. The diagram creates visual interest, but also gives the impression that significant thought has been put into this, and that this is an endeavour of some scale. It makes it look like a big deal.

Keep in mind that InfoSec is often very indoctrinated, very hyped, full of buzzwords, and all of it sounds like hyped-up Greek to C-level management. Except to the Greeks, probably.

It is critical to stand out and to convey the complexity and importance of what will be set in motion by this document. In English.

Page 2:

On this page I create a section that defines the purpose of the document. It generally needs 4 paragraphs.

The first one is brief statement that the Executive Charter aims to capture management support for Information Security in delivering on their mission by defining a clear mandate and by committing the necessary resources.

The second is the Information Security's mission statement. Think your mission statement through thoroughly. You must be aware of your issues and capabilities in order to phrase it to deliver maximum impact where you need it. I like to italicise it.

The third paragraph reaffirms that the charter shows management's proactive commitment (I like to have this word jump off the page in bold) to protect the business from the damaging impact of information loss and systems disruption. It may seem like a repetition of the first but note how we are stating they will protect the business, not support InfoSec.

This has a different and more powerful psychological effect. It is a statement that holds heavier responsibility because it is not an "InfoSec thing", it is their basic duty as senior management. Then we state that they will do so through the approval of a comprehensive Information Security framework and mandating it to all relevant personnel.

What we've done here is made them feel the weight of their information security responsibility, and then given them a way out, a way to simply and easily deal with that responsibility, making them more appreciative of InfoSec and more likely to support InfoSec's efforts.

You've also just gotten your programme formally commissioned, you sneaky devil.

The fourth and final paragraph is a statement about the scope of this charter. Such as "This charter and its directives/statements shall apply to "all Company X" employees, contractors and individuals employed by 3rd parties... (etc., etc.)" This way we define who is in scope, so that they understand that they will have to enforce the statements to everyone, but also that they are not exempt.

Page 3:

This page holds the Charter Statements and Directives. These are the 10 or so directives we covered before, the meat of the charter.

It's quite likely this will spill out into a second page but try to keep the language as tight as possible. Aim for at most 1.5 pages.

Page 4

I title this page "Charter and Framework Approvals." We are making the top brass sign off on this document. It is composed of just one paragraph stating something along the lines of:

The undersigned agree to implement and enforce this charter and the items/directives it contains whether directly or through delegated authority. Such agreement shall remain through evolutionary iterations of the above Charter and mentioned Operational Framework unless explicitly revoked by the undersigned. Any changes will be communicated to the undersigned or their delegates.

Followed by a table with title/position, full name, date, and their signature.

Note that both the section/page title and the blurb *both* mention the framework. It is a quick and easy way of reinforcing to them that they are commissioning something here beyond just the charter, without having to go on and on about it.

I like to take the table with management's signatures and later paste it onto the end of every standard/process document we will create in the framework. It's a reminder that we have support from on high and helps people take processes and procedures more seriously.

A word about tone: When you are writing your statements, be mindful of your tone. The language should be as binding as possible, but also not abrasive.

This is a delicate balance, take care.

The more you build your relationships with the executives that will need to sign off on this charter, the less harsh and more inviting you can make it.

You can also use less binding language in touchy areas such as accountability and funding knowing that you're more likely to reach your goals anyway due to the strength and positive/trusted nature of your relationship with the signatories.

You now have the support to build your framework. It's time to continue building relationships, insights, and knowledge of your organisation and its people, to structure the best and most effective security programme you can.

For them.

This Is the End

I'm going to leave you with an article I wrote back in May of 2019.

I had been unemployed for 7 months at the time (It seems few are those who hire people to fundamentally fix things in security anymore – Most want bodies to work in or manage the parking lot.), but I couldn't help but feel hopeful.

Not for me, not directly anyway, but because I saw seeds germinating. Seeds of the approach, mentality, and sense of duty to do the right thing. Trends I hoped would also, one day, find me in demand again. But really, I was happy to see some sense appearing in the industry.

The article was titled *Hope in InfoSec*, here it is:

There is a lot of negativity in InfoSec. We blame users, we blame senior management, we blame a perceived lack of resources. There's often a sense of technical elitism towards the business, and even towards IT.

I've been doing InfoSec for over 20 years now. Not that many years ago, I was probably guilty of all of the above. I felt like a hotshot and welcomed the industry's FUD (Fear Uncertainty & Doubt)-based marketing so that I could be seen as important and get the budget for the latest security toys. I made beaucoup bucks and suffered from rock star syndrome.

Then, at some point, I grew up. I don't know why exactly. "Old" age, wisdom, fatherhood, and probably a row of terrible toxic bosses that used the FUD to get into positions of power where they served no one but themselves. I didn't want to turn out like them.

I started caring about people, wishing upon no one the toxic "leadership" from the managers and CISOs that had blighted my career. I started thinking about how I would do things if I were in their place.

I began being honest with myself about the fact that the technical work I did, as good as some of it was, wasn't going to fundamentally solve much. And why InfoSec management would turn a blind eye to problems – favouring ego and its own self-interests over protecting the business and its people.

*I started asking why things didn't work, and when I got an answer I asked why again, and again. Eventually I started figuring out the big picture. And I started asking myself if it really was other people's fault, whether I couldn't do things better myself, if I couldn't do **more** and, even when it was partly others' fault, how could I help them? Because I'd started caring, really caring, about the big picture, about the people, and not just about the InfoSec industry and myself.*

I fear the bulk of the security industry is very much where I was 15 years ago. Feeling self-important, wanting all the toys (and budget), snubbing and blaming others (the all too familiar "It's the end-user's fault" or "Management won't listen" excuses), and not really contributing.

Let's get this straight:

- On average I'd say that 80% of operational security effort and spend is on issues that could be eliminated if we engaged the business upstream.

- If someone from marketing lectured us on how we should format our emails to reflect some corporate brand, not even knowing our name, we'd tell them to sod off. – Don't expect people to react differently when you lecture them on security.

- There is no lack of people in InfoSec. There is a lack of addressing issues proactively, resulting in more firefighting. There is a severe lack of mentoring, enablement, accountability, involvement, and care on the part of information security organisations. And there is an excess of overhead and self-serving "busy work".

The real crisis in Information Security is a leadership crisis.

Many InfoSec managers and CISOs are failing to provide even the most basic level of real security, and abysmal value on security spend. A sheer lack of quality and holistic thinking dooms most security programmes and implementations to failure. Sure, the boxes are ticked, but *in most cases what you will find when you lift up the covers will shock you, assuming you understood what you were looking at. Most people wouldn't know, and InfoSec management is all too often willing to exploit that fact.*

We must change how we do InfoSec. We must care, we must engage, we must be real leaders. This means we must be humble, serving, thoughtful, and big-picture individuals that build relationships and listen to every person in the organisation. Only on those relationships can we build the understanding and collaboration to fuse security into the DNA of the organisation, its people, its operations, and its products in a way that is effective.

We need a security culture that is self-reinforcing and negates the need for the ineffective status-quo reactive money-pit we call Information Security today. (Not to mention getting rid of the "security police" - no one likes you.)

I started by talking about negativity, for reasons I've since, fortunately, outgrown. But the reality is I am still negative – just in a different way; because of the fact that we are doing almost everything wrong, and I see the industry running in the wrong direction. I am fearful, and sometimes even depressed because I see vendors' FUD campaigns, empire-building CISOs, standardisation and canned frameworks followed blindly at the expense of real thought and consideration of our organisations' actual needs, and bright people rendered ineffective by poor leaders and theory-induced blindness.

But there might just be hope. A few people are starting to look outside the cyber bubble, seeing and adopting leadership skills from more mature sectors, appreciating the human factors, understanding the importance of culture. Executives are starting to want accountability and visibility. More and more people are listening when there is talk about leadership-based security.

The above make up maybe 1% of the industry, probably less, but I think the seed has been planted. It may be tiny and under a foot of concrete sidewalk, but if we just keep an open mind, it will find a way to break through.

And that's something to be positive about.

P.S. It took me 20 years to get here. Don't be as slow as me.

I hope you found this book helpful. I hope you go on to do great things, things you can feel good about.

All the best,

Greg

Shameless Plugs

I want to give thanks to the amazing team at Sapphire (https://www.sapphire.net) who handle my speaking engagements, courses, and consulting engagements.

#teamtina

If you're interested in my courses, having me speak, or my advisory services, obviously give them a call or simply contact me on LinkedIn.

Speaking of LinkedIn, a huge hello and thanks to all my amazing connections (and friends) on there. You know, for putting up with me!

You know who you are!

Finally, my team and all the great people at UoS.

We may not have much resource, we may have *ahem* "challenges", but it's still a great place to work thanks to you lot.